REDISCOVERING FATIMA

Rediscovering Fatima

by Robert J. Fox

OUR SUNDAY VISITOR, INC.
HUNTINGTON

Contents

Church Endorsements of the Fatima Apparitions

January 17, 1918: the Diocese of Fatima is restored by Pope Benedict XV.

October 13, 1921: the first Mass is celebrated in the Chapel of Apparitions in the Cova da Iria.

1927: a special votive Mass for Our Lady of Fatima is authorized by the Holy See.

October 13, 1930: the bishop of Fatima declares the Fatima apparitions worthy of acceptance as of supernatural origin.

October 31, 1942: Pope Pius XII consecrates the world to the Immaculate Heart of Mary.

May 4, 1944: Pius XII institutes the feast of the Immaculate Heart of Mary, on the twenty-fifth anniversary of the apparitions at Fatima.

May 13, 1946: Pius XII crowns the image of Our Lady of Fatima and proclaims her "Queen of the World."

June 13, 1946: Pius XII issues his encyclical *Deiparae Virginis Mariae*, in which he refers favorably to our Lady's message at Fatima.

October 13, 1951: the Holy Year closing celebration takes place at the Marian shrine in Fatima.

July 7, 1952: Pius XII consecrates the Russian people to the Immaculate Heart of Mary.

October 11, 1954: in his encyclical *Ad Caeli Reginam* (establishing the feast of the Queenship of Mary), Pius XII refers to the miraculous image of Our Lady of Fatima.

November 12, 1954: the sanctuary shrine in Fatima is raised to basilica rank by Pius XII.

October 13, 1956: Pius XII, through papal legate Eugene Cardinal Tisserant, blesses and dedicates the international headquarters of the Blue Army of Our Lady of Fatima, constructed near the shrine in Fatima.

December 13, 1962: Pope John XXIII institutes the feast of Our Lady of the Rosary, in honor of Our Lady of Fatima.

November 21, 1964: Pope Paul VI renews Pius XII's consecration of Russia to the Immaculate Heart, speaking to the Fathers of the Second Vatican Council.

May 13, 1965: Paul VI sends a Golden Rose to Fatima, confiding the "entire Church" to our Lady's protection.

May 13, 1967: Paul VI goes to Fatima, where he calls for renewed consecration to the Immaculate Heart.

May 13, 1982: Pope John Paul II goes to Fatima to pray in thanksgiving for his surviving the attempted assassination on May 13, 1981, and, in union with the bishops of the Church, consecrates the world "collegially" to the Immaculate Heart, renewing the previous acts of consecration by Pius XII (1942, 1952).

 *Foreword*

The pastoral visit of Pope John Paul II to Portugal and to the Shrine of Our Lady of Fatima on May 13, 1982, can be viewed as a call to the world to listen to and practice the message that our Lady gave to three simple shepherd children of Fatima on May 13, 1917, and again during the subsequent months till October 13. Since the time of those appearances of our Lady at Fatima, many books have been written about them. Yet millions of people still remain uninformed about them and fail to catch the spark of Mary's love for all of us and her concern for the spiritual welfare of the world.

This book by Father Fox—*Rediscovering Fatima*—comes at a critical moment in history. The visit of Pope John Paul to Fatima, as well as his manifestation of his deep love for our Blessed Lady, has aroused waves of interest throughout the world, has brought comfort and consolation to souls who have already been touched by the message of Fatima, and has increased their desire to live that message.

Rediscovering Fatima abounds in details concerning the apparitions of the Blessed Mother to the three children in 1917, and it studies most carefully her message calling for conversion and penance. It likewise recalls the subsequent appearances of Mary to Sister Lucia—the only one of the three children alive today—in later years. One could say that this is a source book, one that is needed in these days of a revival of interest in Our Lady of Fatima. The book's title expresses the author's hope that it will help many to "rediscover" the meaning of Fatima.

Why did Pope John Paul decide to visit Fatima? Because of the world war, Pope Pius XII was not able to do so in 1942, on the twenty-fifth anniversary of Mary's first appearance to the shepherd children; instead he broadcast a radio message to the thousands of pilgrims gathered at Fatima. Speaking magnificently and beautifully, he consecrated the world to the Immaculate Heart of Mary. Pope Paul VI similarly showed his love, respect, and support for the truthfulness of this great spiritual blessing by going to Fatima himself on May 13, 1967—the fiftieth anniversary date.

Pope John Paul had two purposes in mind in going to Fatima on May 13, 1982. The first was to express his profound gratitude and appreciation to our loving mother Mary for her having protected him when, on May 13, 1981, an attempt was made to assassinate him. That attempt had been made on the same date and at the same hour when Mary first appeared to the children at Fatima. Pope John Paul has frequently said that Mary's motherly protection was much stronger than the assassin's bullets.

His second reason for going to Fatima was in response to the appeal of thousands that he consecrate the world and Russia to the Immaculate Heart of Mary, together with all the bishops of the world. Prior to his departure from Rome, he had directed Cardinal Casaroli to send a letter to the bishops, informing them that he would renew the Act of Consecration of the world to the Immaculate Heart of Mary, which had first been made by Pope Pius XII on October 31, 1942; and likewise the Act of Consecration of Russia to the Immaculate Heart of Mary, which had originally been made on July 7, 1952. In that letter, Pope John Paul indicated his intention to renew those Acts of Entrusting and Consecration "in spiritual union" with all the bishops. In this way, he fulfilled a request that the Blessed Mother had made to Sister Lucia on June 13, 1929.

Father Fox writes with a strong spirit of conviction, and with deep love in his heart for our Lady. His familiarity with the history of Fatima since the time of the apparitions and his many visits to the shrine there—during which he came to know the relatives of the children very well—provide him with much valuable information and many details which, in general, are not known to all. His book is one to place in the hands of someone who wishes to become acquainted with this Appearance of Mary in the early part of the twentieth century. It is also an inspiring book, a comfort and a consolation to those who may be familiar with the Fatima message and have a great love for it.

May it be the prayer of all that the message of Our Lady of Fatima will become more widely known and lived. The "message" includes so much: chiefly, a call to conversion and repentance; also, recitation of the Rosary daily, the fostering of a spirit of sacrifice in accepting sufferings, the love of the Most Holy Eucharist, the consecration of each person to the Immaculate Heart of Mary, and the faithful practice of observing the First Saturdays over a period of five months (then continuing this practice indefinitely).

What a joy it would be to the world and to individual souls if we would ever seek to know Mary better, to love her more ardently, and to give ourselves totally to her so that she may bring us ever closer to her Divine Son.

John Joseph Cardinal Carberry
ARCHBISHOP OF SAINT LOUIS (RET.)

I.  *Introducing Fatima*

In the second decade of the 20th century, in 1917, the Mother of God appeared to three young children in central Portugal, in the parish of the village of Fatima, north of Lisbon. The parish church is dedicated to St. Anthony of Padua; the name of the village is of Muslim origin, a reminder that the Iberian peninsula had once been in the control of the followers of Mohammed. Fatima was the name of Mohammed's sister.

About a mile and a half to the west of Fatima, still within the parish boundaries, is the Cova da Iria ("cove of Irene"). Some say the cove was named after St. Irene of Portugal (d. 653); others say that there used to be a chapel dedicated to St. Irene on the site, or that the land was once owned by a woman named Irene. In any case, it was in the Cova da Iria that the Virgin Mary—Our Lady of Fatima—appeared to the three children on six occasions between May 13 and October 13, 1917.

The holm-oak tree—a shrub-size evergreen species—above which the Virgin appeared to the children is gone now, and in its place stands the Capelinha ("little chapel"), or Chapel of Apparitions. The Cova has become a mecca for millions of pilgrims from all over the world. But the Cova as it was in 1917 is no longer visible. A beautiful basilica has been constructed there; and visitors may experience a sense of disappointment unless they come already informed about the events that happened there in 1917 *and* about their meaning.

i

I have celebrated Mass on several occasions with Sister Lucia (Lucia Santos) present. She was one of the three children who witnessed the Virgin's appearances. The other two children, Francisco and Jacinto Marto, Lucia's cousins, died shortly after experiencing the apparitions. I have met with surviving members of all their families, who still live in the hamlet of Aljustrel, barely a mile distant from St. Anthony of Padua Church in Fatima.

John Marto, brother of Francisco and Jacinto, and now in his seventies, recognizes me immediately each year as I arrive to spend the greater part of the summer in Fatima. He and Maria dos Anjos, Lucia's sister, now in her nineties, have welcomed my visits and reminisced freely with me concerning the events of 1917. Those events have gained the attention of the world, but have left the simplicity of their life untouched.

John Marto and his wife, Amelia, still live in the house where Jacinto and Francisco lived at the time of the apparitions. The physical poverty of their household is hard to believe, measured by "modern" standards; yet they are richly happy.

The house has been little changed. Jacinta's room, with its small bed, is the same as it was in 1917; and in Francisco's room stands the bed in which he died. Around the bend from their house is Lucia's family house, also unchanged. In her bedroom still hangs a crucifix that she once had Jacinta kiss instead of kissing her brother after she lost a game of forfeits. Around the fireplace, Lucia's mother, Maria Rosa, used to gather her children on winter evenings to tell them stories that illustrated their religious faith. There too is the spinning wheel that Lucia especially asked be kept in her family home, as a remembrance of the family's activities.

Behind the Santos house is the well (see page 81) where the children played in the shade of the fig trees. The branches of one of the trees served them as a swing. At the well, an angel appeared to them; at the well, they used to meet for colloquies and prayer. As Lucia described it in her memoirs, the well is "hidden by some chestnut trees, a clump of stones and brambles." The "prayer cells" that have been formed by young people with a devotion to Our Lady of Fatima have as their model the meetings of Jacinta, Francisco, and Lucia in the privacy of the well-site, where they discussed the visions they had received and prayed as they had been asked by the angel and the Lady.

Visitors commonly drink of the water from that well. Lucia wrote of it: "We mixed our tears with the well's water and drank them later from the same fountain where we had shed them. Wouldn't that cistern be a figure of Mary, in whose heart we dried our weeping and drank the most pure consolation?"

Few visitors to the Cova da Iria are aware that the surviving family members of the three children have continued to live in nearby Aljustrel in the same manner as they had lived in 1917. Of those who make the side-trip to Aljustrel, to visit the homes of the children, few are aware that family members still live in them. The latter do not identify themselves unless asked; they take no worldly pride in their relationship to the three children whom heaven chose to be bearers of a message to the world.

Recognizing that in a few more years' time, the remaining survivors who could recall the events of 1917 would no longer be available, I have, in recent years, interviewed them so that their testimony as witnesses would not be lost to later generations. From time to time, I will refer to that testimony, in their own words.

ii

The terrain of central Portugal is rocky, its soil poor. It takes a great deal of hard work to farm the land. Summers are dry; it seldom rains; forest fires in the vicinity of Fatima are not uncommon. The people still live a peasant life, largely dependent on the land for food and income. Olive oil is the chief marketable commodity for them; and it is especially tragic when (as happened in 1981) fire destroys large numbers of olive trees. (There is some evidence that at least some fires are deliberately set. Communist agitators are suspected to be to blame.)

In June, the farmers harvest wheat; in early fall, maize and grapes. Vineyards produce wine. In August of each year, on the 13th, hundreds of farmers bring sacks of wheat to the basilica at the Cova da Iria, to donate for use in making flour for altar breads. These breads will be consecrated and distributed in Holy Communion at Masses celebrated during the coming year, to the millions of pilgrims who will come to Fatima. The women who accompany the men in the ceremony of wheat-giving carry sacks of the grain atop their heads, climbing the many stairs that lead to the entrance of the basilica. The basilica itself—the Basilica of Our Lady of the Rosary—stands atop the hill where Jacinta, Francisco, and Lucia played their games while herding their sheep.

Along the roads leading to Fatima, it is common to see a peasant with his donkey and cart. In the fall, the cart may be filled with grapes; in the summer, with hay, or perhaps a pig or goat being taken to market. The donkey carts share the same, narrow highways with fast-moving automobiles. Many of the cars are from other countries; in central Portugal, few people own cars. The highways become particularly dangerous in August, when young Portuguese men who have gone to France to work during the summer return home. Speed limits, if they exist at all, are not enforced. It is quite a contrast to see the automobile drivers reluctantly sharing the highways and roads leading to Fatima with the donkey carts and the pilgrims traveling on foot.

The peasant farmers of Portugal have no modern agricultural machinery. They work the fields in the same manner as their predecessors in earlier centuries. Yet I have found in them a wealth unknown to those whose treasures are made up of that which moth and rust consume. In them I have discovered something of the "spirit" of Fatima, especially in those hundreds of thousands who come from the hamlets, valleys, and mountainsides of Portugal, in pilgrimage each year to Fatima. Foreign visitors to Fatima do not always come in the same "spirit."

I have noticed also that American visitors to Portugal are inclined to look askance at the ways in which the Portuguese people accomplish their tasks. Many are unable to read in the faces of the Portuguese pilgrims two riches: their families, and their faith. Little children, babes in arms, teenagers, young men and women, the very old—they all come, they all pray. Many "walk" on their knees down the long "penitential path" that begins near the tall iron cross at the entrance to the Cova and leads to the Chapel of Apparitions.

Many years ago, returning from one of my early pilgrimages to Fatima, I was interviewed on television in one of the major cities in the United States. Asked to say what impressed me most about Fatima, I replied, "The people."

It was that way then. It is that way still—though I have, over the years, grown more accustomed to their ways and now take them more for granted. Yet in these millions of people making their way each year to Fatima, I continue to feel a magnetic pull. At Fatima, I sense the moral presence of God's Mother. There, one sees miracles of grace.

iii

In 1981, a counselor who assisted me with the annual young men's pilgrimage to Fatima—an Irish seminarian named Sean Brown—advised them: "Scoop up all the graces here. If you go home with only a suitcase full of souvenirs, you will have missed everything. . . . The real 'buys' are at the Cova. If you spend your time there, you will go home with something valuable." Sean followed his own advice. Ten days after our pilgrimage ended, he died; and I have no doubt that Our Lady welcomed him into heaven. At Fatima, he had made his consecration to his guardian angel. "My guardian angel is with me not only at all times on earth," he had said, "but he will be with me for all eternity to adore God with me. Our angels won't help us in this life unless we ask them to."

I have seen countless numbers of young people transformed at Fatima. I've seen many of them in tears while they made a general confession. The tears came not only from sorrow but also from joy at being touched by the grace they have received through the intercession of the Immaculate Heart of Mary.

Late one evening, near midnight, I came out of the Fatima chapel's confessional and noticed a young man—he was about 19 years old—in tears. "Whatever are you crying for?" I asked him. "Because the other guys have found Mary, and I can't find her," he said. I assured him that his tears were a gift and a sign that he had not only "found" Mary but had been touched by a special grace.

Pope Pius XII, in a radio broadcast many years ago, spoke of the abundant graces available to pilgrims to the Cova. I have found that it is so. Many of the young men who have accompanied me to Fatima have received a call to the priesthood; and many young women, a call to the religious life. They too are impressed by "the people." The sight of so many thousands of pilgrims coming to Fatima *on foot* is a testimony of faith that the young people cannot resist. There is a large tent set up in the Cova as a first-aid station; there, nurses tend to the pilgrims' swollen, bleeding feet. The young people think, "If they love our Lord and our Lady so much, why not I?"

iv

On the evening of the 12th and on the morning of the 13th of the month, May through October, the statue of Our Lady of Fatima—the one used when pilgrims first started coming to the Cova—is carried in procession. The statue is taken from its usual place atop the pillar inside the Capelinha—the pillar marking the spot where the little holm-oak tree once stood—and placed on a carrier. Flowers are banked around the foot of the statue, and four strong men serve as bearers. On a number of occasions, I have seen doves land at the feet of the statue during the procession. The bearers take the statue to the entranceway of the Cova and then make their way through the center of the "white square" that stands in front of the basilica; they circle the fountain and its miraculous water. (In the center of the fountain is a pillar on which stands a large, bronze statue representing the Sacred Heart of Jesus.) The procession then moves up the steps of the basilica, and the statue is placed beside the main altar, where solemn Mass is then sung.

The procession has this symbolism: the faithful are led by Mary to the altar where Mass is celebrated and where thousands receive Holy Communion. This is the role of Mary—leading us in faith to her Son, Jesus Christ.

During the early years following the apparitions of 1917, many miracles were reported as associated with the statue of Our Lady of Fatima. During the processions in the Cova, those who move the statue from pillar to carrier wear gloves to protect it from soiling; each night, at 10:30, it is removed from the open-air Capelinha and placed in an indoor location until morning.

v

Standing beneath the open skies in the Cova da Iria, the pilgrim looks upward and recalls that this is where, at exactly high noon on October 13, 1917, between seventy- and a hundred-thousand people had come to see whether the miracle that the Lady had reportedly told the children about would take place. It did.

Dark clouds hung over Fatima; they had covered the Cova since the evening before. Rain, swept by strong wind, beat upon the faces of the people, soaking to the bone those who had no protection. Suddenly, exactly at noon, the flash of lighting that had always preceded the Lady's apparitions occurred. A little later, Lucia cried out, "Look at the sun." The clouds swept back. The rain stopped. The sun appeared. The people could look easily at the sun; it did not blind or hurt their eyes to do so. The sun was seen spinning like a giant Catherine-wheel, turning on itself, shooting off rays of different colors, painting everything—the trees, the people, the air, the ground. The colors would be yellow, then blue, then red, then white, and so on. It seemed as though the wheel of fire might fall upon the people. Many cried out for God's mercy, thinking the end of the world had surely come.

People fell on their knees on the muddy ground. People wept and prayed aloud. The sun trembled and made movements that defied all cosmic laws. "The sun danced" was a typical description given by those who witnessed the miracle—not only in the Cova but for 30-some miles around.

Three times the sun had performed its movements and returned to its orbit.

When the miracle was over, the people rejoiced that they were still alive, and that the end of the world had not really come. Then, suddenly, when their excitement began to die down, they noticed that everyone, and everything, was dry.

In her first apparition to the children, the Lady had said, "Continue to come here every month. In October I will tell you who I am and what I want, and I will perform a miracle so that all may believe." When the stupendous miracle was accomplished, the people believed that God's Mother had truly been appearing to Jacinta, Francisco, and Lucia. The Lady had kept her word. Many who witnessed the event are still alive; and I have had the privilege of hearing their accounts of "the day the sun danced."

vi

What was the Santos family like, which gave us Lucia? What was the Marto family like, which gave us Jacinta and her brother Francisco?

Antonios Santos, Lucia's father, seemed to lack some firmness of character; and for a time he had difficulties with the parish priest. Yet his attitudes were basically religious. Maria Rosa, his wife, conpensated for his instability by making special efforts to educate and form her children in Christian virtue.

Maria dos Anjos, Lucia's oldest sister, once told me: "Our mother knew how to read printed letters but could not write. Every night during the winter, she used to read us some part of the Old Testament or the Gospels, or some story of Our Lady of Nazaré or Lourdes. I clearly remember her saying crossly to Lucia at the time of the apparitions: 'Do you think that because Our Lady appeared in Nazaré and in Lourdes, she has to appear to you?'

"In Lent we knew that the readings would be about the Passion of Our Lord. Afterward, Lucia would give her own account to the other children. Mother taught us doctrine and would not let us go and play until we knew it properly by heart. She did not want to feel ashamed, she said, when the parish priest examined us. And she had no need to be, for the priest was very pleased with us and, even when we were quite small, used to let us teach other children in church. I could not have been more than nine when he made me a catechist. But Mother was never satisfied with our just saying the words, and explained everything so that we should understand it well. She used to say that repeating catechism without knowing the meaning of it was worse than useless. We used to ask her all sorts of questions, and she explained even better than the priest in church. One day I asked her how it was that the fire of hell did not destroy the damned like the wood in the fire. She asked us if we had not seen a bone thrown into the fire and how it seemed to burn without being destroyed. This rather frightened us, and we made firm resolutions not to sin and fall into that terrible fire.

"But it was not only to us that mother taught catechism. Other children, and even grown-up people, used to come to our house to have lessons.

"In May, and in the month of the Holy Souls, also in Lent, we used to say the Rosary every day at the fireside; and when we went out with the flocks, mother always used to remind us to take a rosary in our pockets. 'Remember,' she would tell us, 'to say your beads to Our Lady after lunch, and some Our Fathers to St. Anthony to keep the sheep from getting lost.' We also used to say: 'All honor and thanks to Our Lord Jesus Christ, for the grace and blessing He has given us and will give us.' We would always add some prayers for the souls we knew in purgatory. Night and morning we would make an Act of Contrition and invoke our guardian angel, as well as say several Our Fathers."

Lucia, born March 22, 1907, was the youngest of seven children; her cousins Francisco and Jacinta Marto, younger than Lucia, were themselves the youngest in their family. Jacinta and Francisco were, respectively, the sixth and seventh children of their father and the eighth and ninth of their mother, who had borne two children before her first husband died. Jacinta was born March 11, 1910, and Francisco on June 11, 1908.

Manuel Pedro Marto—commonly known as Ti Marto—was as talkative as Antonio Santos was quiet. While Ti Marto did not put emphasis on reading and writing, he believed in educating his children wisely. He once described his household this way:

"They say that our house was always quiet. And yet we had nine youngsters! I liked things to be as they should be. I remember once a certain person came to the house on some errand or another and the children would chatter and hinder me. I didn't say anything at the time, but afterward I gave them a scolding and it never happened again. After that, when anyone came to the house, they all went out into the street. A look was enough. That wasn't always necessary. If a donkey kicks, you needn't cut off its leg!

"Once Francisco refused to say his prayers and hid in the out-kitchen. I went to him, and when he saw me coming he cried out at once that he would pray! That was before Our Lady appeared. After that he never failed to say his prayers. In fact he and Jacinta would almost force us to say the Rosary."

Ti Marto and his wife, Olimpia, were inclined to believe their children's reports of the apparitions from the first; but they were very cautious in speaking of them to others. While Antonio Santos kept a reserved silence about Lucia's reports of the events, his wife, Maria Rosa, was militant in her efforts to get Lucia to admit the whole thing was a lie, taking the broom after her on at least one occasion, and dragging the child off to the priest to confess that she had lied in claiming that the Lady from heaven had appeared to her. Whatever weaknesses Antonio may have had, Lucia loved him very much; she was crushed when he died (1919). Years later, she recalled that it was her father who gave her the most support when the others in her family seemed to turn against her after their farm and garden land in the Cova were destroyed by the rush of curiosity-seekers who had heard reports of visions there.

If anyone needed a miracle to be convinced that a "beautiful Lady from heaven" was appearing in the Cova on the 13th of each month, at the hour of noon, it was Maria Rosa Santos. She was no doubt the last one in Aljustrel and Fatima to believe that the Lady had actually appeared to the children. Although Lucia suffered terribly because of the disbelief of her mother, years later, writing from her convent cell, she could see the design of heaven in her mother's initial reaction, making the authenticity of the apparitions more credible to the world, and forming Lucia herself in needed virtue. Only after the "miracle of the sun" did Maria Rosa believe.

At the very first apparition, on May 13, 1917, and in each succeeding apparition in the Cova, Lucia asked the Lady, "What do you want of me?" At the first apparition, the Lady had answered: "I came to ask you to come here for six successive months, on the 13th day at the same hour. Later I will tell you what I want."

The children were informed by God's Mother, during her first appearance, that sufferings would accomplish their mission. But as heaven always respects human freedom in bestowing special vocations, she asked them: "Do you wish to offer up to God all the sufferings He desires to send you in reparation for the sins by which He is offended, and in supplication for the conversion of sinners?"

"Yes, we do."

"Go then, for you will have much to suffer, but the grace of God will comfort you."

While pronouncing the words "the grace of God," our Lady opened her hands for the first time, shedding on the children a light so intense that it seemed like a reflex glancing from her hands and penetrating to the inmost depths of their hearts, enabling them to see themselves in God, who was that light. "We could see ourselves more clearly," says Lucia, "than we could see ourselves in a mirror. Then, by an interior impulse, also communicated to us, we fell upon our knees, repeating in our hearts: 'Oh, most Holy Trinity, I adore you! My God, my God, I love you in the most Blessed Sacrament!'"

After a few moments, our Lady spoke again, making a request for praying the Rosary daily—something she did during each of the six apparitions. "Say the Rosary every day in order to obtain peace for the world and the end of the war [World War I]."

Then the Lady began to ascend serenely, going up toward the east; the light that surrounded her seemed to open up a path before her, until she finally disappeared in the immensity of space—the reason the children sometimes said that they saw "heaven opening."

An angel who had appeared three times to the children in the previous year—1916—had already initiated the children into the basic message of

Fatima, which God's Mother was to develop profoundly in their tender hearts, to be spread from them to the world.

"The "basic message" of Fatima is reparation, especially Eucharistic reparation. This reparation involves prayer, penance, a turning away from sin, and a turning toward the supreme sacrifice of Jesus Christ on the cross as perpetuated in the Holy Eucharist.

Mary not only asked the children, each time, to pray the Rosary daily, but taught them to pray it properly, meditating on the mysteries of Christ. Meditating on those mysteries of Christ is excellent preparation for Eucharistic reparation; it is also a thanksgiving or an echo of the Mass, which is Christ's sacrifice renewed.

In the spring of 1916, the angel had identified himself to the children as "the Angel of Peace." At that time, the spirit of atheism, personified in Communism, was beginning to take firm hold of a world growing ever more materialistic. The angel invited the children to repeat with him their faith in God.

Appearing to them as a young man about 15 years of age, transparent and brighter than crystal pierced by the rays of the sun, kneeling down, the angel bowed his countenance to the ground. By a similar supernatural impulse, the children imitated him and repeated the words they heard him pronounce:

"My God, I believe, I adore, I trust, and I love you. I beg pardon for those who do not believe, do not adore, do not trust, and do not love you."

After repeating these same words three times, the Angel of Peace rose and said: "Pray like this. The Hearts of Jesus and Mary are attentive to the voice of your supplications."

When the angel disappeared, a "supernatural atmosphere" enveloped the children so intensely that for hours they were scarcely aware of their own existence, remaining in the same position and repeating the same prayers over and over.

So intense was their sense of the presence of God that the three children could not speak to each other; only gradually did it fade away in the following days. They had no need to caution each other not to report to others the apparitions of the angel. Jacinta and Francisco went to their graves without mentioning them. Only years later, after the Church (in 1930) officially approved the apparitions of Mary in the Cova da Iria, did Lucia reveal the angel's earlier apparitions.

Lucia wrote: "The very apparition itself seemed to impose silence on us. It was of such an intimate nature that it was not easy to speak of it at all. Perhaps because it was the first such manifestation, it made a greater impression on us."

About mid-summer of 1917, the angel appeared to the three children again, saying: "Pray! Pray a great deal! The Hearts of Jesus and Mary have designs of mercy for you. Offer up prayers and sacrifices to the Most High."

"How are we to make sacrifices?" Lucia asked.

"Make everything you do a sacrifice, and offer it as an act of reparation for

the sins by which He is offended, and in supplication for the conversion of sinners. Bring peace to your country in this way. I am its Angel Guardian, the
Angel of Portugal. Above all, accept and bear with submission the sufferings
sent you by Our Lord."

Lucia writes that the words of the angel, in his second apparition, "made a
deep impression on our minds, like a light asking us to understand who God is,
how He loves us and desires to be loved, as well as the value of sacrifice, how
pleasing it is to Him, and how, on account of it, He grants the grace of conversion to sinners. For this reason, from that moment we began to offer up all
that mortified us, never seeking other ways of mortification and penance, except to remain for hours, with our foreheads touching the ground, repeating
the prayer the Angel had taught us."

At the third angelic apparition, either in October or toward the end of
September (Lucia was never certain of the exact date)—while the children
were at Loco do Cabeço, a hillside near Aljustrel and Casa Velha, overlooking
the hamlet of Aljustrel—the angel gave Jacinta and Francisco their first Holy
Communion. (Lucia had already been privileged to receive her First Communion at the age of six in her parish church, many years younger than the age normally permitted in those days.) Holding in his hands a chalice surmounted by a
host, from which some drops of precious blood were falling into the chalice,
and then leaving the chalice and host suspended in the air, the angel prostrated
himself on the ground, saying three times: "Most Holy Trinity, Father, Son,
and Holy Spirit, I adore you profoundly. I offer you the most precious Body,
Blood, Soul, and Divinity of Jesus Christ, present in all the tabernacles of the
world, in reparation for the outrages, sacrileges, and indifference by which He
is offended. And through the infinite merits of the Sacred Heart of Jesus and
the Immaculate Heart of Mary, I beg the conversion of poor sinners."

Rising, the angel took the chalice and the host, giving the host to Lucia and
the contents of the chalice to Jacinta and Francisco, saying at the same time:
"Take and drink the Body and Blood of Jesus Christ, horribly outraged by un-
grateful men. Repair their crimes and console your God."

Prostrating himself on the ground once again, the Angel repeated the prayer
to the Holy Trinity three times. The children felt supernaturally impelled to
imitate the angel in all that he did.

The effect of this Eucharistic presence and reception of Holy Communion
from the angel was so intense, in the sense of the presence of God, that, being
completely overwhelmed and absorbed by it, for many days thereafter, the
children had the impression that their physical actions were impelled by a supernatural being. While inwardly they felt a great peace and joy, with their
souls entirely immersed in God, yet they felt physically exhausted. "I do not
know why," Lucia later wrote, "but the effect produced by the apparitions of
Our Lady was very different. We would feel the same inward joy, the same

peace and happiness, but instead of physical exhaustion, there was a sense of expansion and alacrity; instead of this annihilation in the Divine Presence, we felt an exultant joy; instead of a difficulty in speaking, a certain communicative enthusiasm."

The explanation for that difference may be that while Mary is greater than all the angels and saints combined, she is still of our human nature and the angels are not. Mary is the Queen of man and angel alike. That is, she is the greatest of all human and angelic creatures. She is both human and spiritual to the greatest possible degree next to Jesus Christ. Being of both worlds, human, originally conceived as a human being on earth, and now above the angels in dignity as God's Mother, our Blessed Lady has a unique place in God's plan for His creation. The angel who appeared to the children of Fatima prepared for that which Mary perfected.

vii

The pilgrim to Fatima wisely spends time in prayer and silence at the Loca do Cabeço, where the first and third apparitions of the angel took place, and where the little shepherds loved to pray and make their sacrifices in secret. Today, one finds at the Cabeço a commemorative shrine, in which statues of the children are placed among the large rocks before a statue of the Angel of Peace, shown holding a host and chalice. (The statue of the angel has no wings; Lucia described the angel as having the appearance of a young man, without wings.)

On the same hill called the Cabeço, the pilgrim will find the *Via Sacra* and Chapel of Saint Stephen. The fourteen Stations of the Cross are placed along the path the children used to follow as they took their sheep to the Cova. The stations, chapel, and a large Calvary, complete with characters of the crucifixion scene, were erected by Hungarian Catholics who had been sheltered in the free nations during World War I. Known as the "Hungarian Calvary of Cardinal Mindszenty," the shrine was inaugurated on May 12, 1964.

Returning to the Cova da Iria, one discovers more there than the vast open plaza, capable of holding one million people; on some occasions, there have been millions more spilling over from the Cova and down the access roads. One such occasion was the Golden Jubilee celebration, May 13, 1967, when Pope Paul VI came to Fatima as a pilgrim to pray for peace in the world and in the Church.

Jacinta, only 7 years old at the time of the apparitions of 1917, could never understand why the Holy Father did not come to Fatima. She must have been pleased, looking down from heaven, on that May 13, 1967, when television cameras were focused on the Cova da Iria, and millions around the world saw Pope Paul present Sister Lucia to the pilgrims. With a gesture of his hands, he said (as Bishop John Vanancio interpreted for me at the time): "What she stands for, I support."

Pope Paul's pilgrimage to Fatima has been commemorated by a statue near the Cova entrance, showing him on his knees, looking toward the basilica. Nearby, on the north side of the square, is another monument, to Pope Pius XII, built by means of offerings given by German Catholics. This Pope—a promoter of devotions to Mary—reportedly saw the miracle of the spinning of the sun as he walked in the Vatican gardens.

A third monument is dedicated to Dom Jose Alves Correia da Silva, Bishop of Leiria; it was erected on the centenary of his birth, 1972. He first approved the Fatima apparitions as worthy of belief. He suffered much under the evils of his day, not only mentally but physically. His mortal remains rest in the basilica chancel; and one sees the front of his tomb as one kneels at the altar rail.

Standing in the square, facing the basilica, one is reminded of St. Peter's Square in Rome. Long wings of colonnades sweep to left and right in a curve, as if to embrace the hundreds of thousands of pilgrims who come to stand before it. The four main figures on the colonnades, forming a guard of honor, are Portuguese heroes of sanctity: St. John of God, St. John Brito, St. Anthony of Lisbon, and Blessed Nuno of Santa Maria. There are other statues of saints, including St. John Bosco, St. Dominic Savio, St. Louis Maria Grignon de Monfort, St. Alphonsus de Liguori, St. John Baptist de La Salle, St. Ignatius of Loyola, St. Francis de Sales, St. Vincent de Paul, St. Simon Stock, St Paul of the Cross, Blessed Marcelino Champagnat, St. Teresa of Avila, and St. John of the Cross.

The basilica, with its 65-meter-high tower, is surmounted by a crown of bronze weighing seven tons and by a large crystal cross, which is lighted during the nighttime services. Every 15 minutes, the basilica chimes ring out the "Fatima Ave," which can be heard even as one prays at the Cabeço or walks the streets of Aljustrel, a mile and a half away. The basilica was dedicated on October 7, 1953.

Entering the basilica, one first notices the painting above the high altar depicting Our Lady coming down to the little shepherds, they having been prepared by the Angel of Peace through their encounter with Christ in the Holy Eucharist. The same composite painting shows the bishop of the diocese kneeling on the left side; Pope Pius XII, who crowned the statue of Our Lady of Fatima, proclaiming her "Queen of the World," and who consecrated the world to the Immaculate Heart of Mary; Pope John XXIII, who, after having visited the sanctuary before his election to the papacy, gave a Marian orientation to Vatican Council II, authorized the feast of Our Lady of Fatima (May 13), and named her patroness of the diocese of Leiria-Fatima; and Pope Paul VI, who declared Mary, Mother of God, to be also Mother of the Church.

Just to the side of the sanctuary, but to the front of the basilica, are the statues of the special saint-apostles of the Rosary and of devotion to the Immaculate Heart of Mary: St. Anthony M. Claret and St. Dominic. There are images also of St. John Eudes and St. Stephen, King of Hungary. Some niches are still empty—perhaps, as some think, reserved for the day when the three children have their sanctity affirmed by the Church.

Pilgrims are drawn eventually to the tombs holding the remains of Francisco and Jacinta, in the right and left transepts, respectively. When the remains of Francisco were removed from the Fatima cemetery to the basilica, only bones and a bit of hair were found in the coffin. The body of Jacinta, twice exhumed, was found to be incorrupt.

viii

Many attempts have been made to explain or summarize the "message of Fatima." A leaflet distributed to the pilgrims in the basilica offers this brief statement:

> *The words of our Lady to the three little children were not for them only but for us, and although years have gone by since they were first spoken, they continue to be an inexhaustible fountain of sound spiritual doctrine. As for the world at large, the Message of Fatima pleads with sinners to stop offending God, to obtain pardon for their sins and to amend their lives, as did the prodigal of the Gospel; it asks the just to pray much and to make sacrifices for sinners and to keep souls from going to hell; all are to recite the Rosary every day, to know and love our Lady, to have devotion to her Immaculate Heart, and to receive Communion in reparation on the first Saturday of the month.*
>
> *If people do not do these things, Russia will spread her errors throughout the world, causing wars and persecutions against the Church. Many will be martyred, the Holy Father (the Pope) will have much to suffer, several nations will be annihilated. Each of us can use world events as the foundation of his judgment as to whether or not people are fulfilling the Message of Fatima.*
>
> *We have our Blessed Mother's own words to assure us of peace and happiness for the entire world, if people do what she has requested of them, when she appeared at Fatima in 1917.*

The traveler who "stops off" at Fatima for a few hours or a day is likely to say, "I've been to Fatima. There's nothing there." The *pilgrim* who stays to pray, to meditate, and to absorb the spirit of Eucharistic reparation, upon leaving, declares, "I must go back again." Many have returned year after year from throughout the world. For them, Fatima is going "back home," where they rediscover their Mother.

Just as Jesus chose a small nation in which to bring His revelation to the world nearly 2000 years ago, His mother likewise chose, at Fatima, the small nation of Portugal as the place where she would reaffirm the gospel. "Europe's Garden by the Sea," it has long been called. Devout Catholics sometimes call it

"Our Lady's Land." Historians refer to it as the European nation with the longest continuous history. In area it measures only 92,082 sq. km (35,553 sq. mi.)—slightly larger than the state of Maine. Its 1980 population was 9,866,000. Yet the Portuguese language is spoken by more than a hundred million people. Using the seas as its highway. Portugal once acquired worldwide dominions. Its empire has waned, but the Portuguese influence—not least its spiritual influence because of Fatima—is still felt throughout the world.

Fatima, located in Portugal's mountainous central region of the Serra de Aire, about thirty miles from the Atlantic Ocean, was all but unknown in 1917; when the apparitions began, the world ignored them, as it has largely ignored the Lady's message. As mankind experiences the final decades of the 20th century and looks toward the 21st centry, the world is only beginning to discover (or rediscover) the message of Our Lady of Fatima, and to see that it is a message for the entire world. The message was so simple that people could not grasp its significance. The Lady's prophecies have been gradually fulfilled with each passing decade, and many are beginning to restudy and rethink so as to discover the depth of her message—which can be discerned best by those willing to pray and become as little children.

Articles in *National Geographic*, in *GEO The Earth Diary*, and in other widely circulated magazines have given sympathetic attention to Fatima in recent years. The skepticism that initially greeted reports of apparitions of Mary in both Lourdes and Fatima seems to be giving way to respect for, if not acceptance of, the evidence of physical-moral cures associated with them.

The visitor to Lourdes is easily impressed by the size of the basilica (second largest in the world) and by the Lourdes water. The visitor to Fatima finds a relatively small basilica, overlooking the site of the apparitions. The field as it once appeared in the Cova da Iria, and the small oak above which Mary appeared to Francisco, Jacinta, and Lucia, are no longer to be seen. If they still existed as they were in 1917, tourists would probably find them disappointingly ordinary. When it became necessary to level off the Cova and pave its surface to accommodate the millions of pilgrims, the bishop of Fatima stood looking over the site with a heavy heart. It was necessary—but not all that is necessary is necessarily easy for human emotions to accept. If Fatima is today called the "world's largest Marian shrine," it is only because of its vast open square, which can hold at least a million pilgrims. Fatima is a shrine to which the pilgrim needs to come in faith and respond in love.

In a sense, the shrine of Fatima takes in an area with a two-mile radius, with the Cova da Iria as its center. It includes the Fatima parish church, where the children were baptized, and where Lucia, kneeling before the small statue of our Lady, saw the Lady smile at her on the day of her First Communion. This statue—hardly a thing of beauty—is still in the church, as is the large mural portraying Our Lady of Mt. Carmel in a form that Lucia described as resembling the Lady of the apparitions. But then, Our Lady of Sameira in Braga, northern Portugal, was also described by the children as resembling the "beautiful Lady from heaven." Years later, Sister Lucia told the American priest-sculptor Thomas McGlynn, O.P., as he made a model of the Immaculate Heart according to her detailed descriptions, "No matter how beautiful you make it, it will never be as beautiful as our Lady."

Lucia could describe the Lady only as being "all light." Today one can see a white-marble statue placed in the niche above the entrance to the basilica. Sculpted by Father McGlynn, it looks out over the Cova. This Lady of the Immaculate Heart is holding her hands in the positions as the children saw them when she first appeared to them and said, "God wishes to establish in the world devotion to my Immaculate Heart."

The pilgrim visiting the Fatima parish church can recall how the children spent the winter months following the apparitions of the angel, in deep prayer and penance, unaware of the forthcoming visits of God's Mother and the suffering that would follow. "The Hearts of Jesus and Mary have designs of mercy for you," the angel had said. "Offer up prayers and sacrifices to the Most High." Jacinta and Francisco had received their first Holy Communion from the Angel in the Loca do Cabeço ("Cabeço" meaning simply "head," head of the hill or mountain as it overlooked the village of Aljustrel). The landscape surrounding the Cabeço is unchanged from the way it appeared in 1917. I have taken more than a thousand young Americans to the spot and spent up to a half hour with them there in silent prayer, the only sounds being of birds singing, or crickets chirping, or a dog barking in the distance. Silence. It is what the angels enjoy.

The parish of St. Anthony's, more than 400 years old, retains the baptismal font in which Jacinta, Francisco, and Lucia were baptized. In this church, Francisco, knowing he would die soon, and rather than go to school to learn to read and write, would often spend his days in meditation before the "hidden Jesus," the Eucharistic Lord, in the Blessed Sacrament. Often he would go right up and place his little arms on the altar, as close as he could get to the tabernacle. In this same House of God, Our Lady of Fatima appeared to Jacinta, showing her tableaux of the 15 mysteries of the Rosary, teaching her how to meditate on the mysteries, so that she could pray the Rosary "properly."

When Jacinta was sick unto death, knowing from the Lady that her days were limited, and confined to her bedroom in Aljustrel, she would long for visits from Lucia. While unable to go to Mass herself, Jacinta would ask Lucia, upon returning from Mass, to come sit close by her. This oldest of the Fatima children, who had been promised she would spend years upon earth to spread devotion to the Immaculate Heart of Mary, had just received the "hidden Jesus" into her soul; in this way Jacinta would feel close to her Eucharistic Lord, revealed so clearly to all three children at the Cabeço.

To those people who have come to Fatima and whose first impression is disappointment ("There is nothing here—well, almost nothing"), I have given this advice: "There is much here. You must look for it. You must pray. You must meditate. I've been coming here every year for years. I've been studying Fatima for over a quarter of a century, and still I have much more to learn and to discover here." Years later, some write to thank me for orienting them away from sight-seeing and toward meditated prayer.

ix

Portugal's location places it as the nation closest to the New World, as part of the Iberian peninsula; and its Altantic coastline, facing west, also looks south to the great sea routes to Africa. The nation is so old that no one knows for certain who founded its capital city of Lisbon, but some sources say Lisbon's name belongs to the hero of *The Odyssey*. On several medieval maps, what is now Portugal bears the name Olissibona, meaning "Ulysses the good."

Portugal has suffered numerous invasions—from the Romans, the Suevians, the Visigoths, the Moors, and the Spaniards. There are many races combined in the Portuguese people; they don't have to deal with ethnic problems; and as combinations of ethnics, they are a beautiful people for the Mother of all races to choose to be recipients of a message for the world.

Fatima, a name with strong associations with the Moorish occupation of Portugal and with the religion of Islam, reminds me that the people of Islam honor Fatima, the prophet Mohammed's sister, but that they also honor the mother of Jesus—although they do not believe that her Son is the eternal Son of God become man. Some think that Our Lady of Fatima will be an instrument for the conversion of the millions of people of Islamic faiths.

The Moors occupied the southern portion of Portugal for more than 500 years, until the middle of the 13th century. To the present day, the Moorish influence is strong in the south; the practice of the Catholic faith is strong in central and northern Portugal. Of the major cities, Porto is an industrial town; Braga is known as the Rome of Portugal; Coimbra claims the country's university; while Lisbon, to the south, is the nation's capital. In Portugal there is a saying: "In Porto they work, in Braga they pray; in Coimbra they study, and in Lisbon they play."

In 1974, the conservative dictatorship ended in Portugal. In that same year, during my annual visit to Fatima, I found the hammer and sickle, symbols of Communism, throughout the land, painted on the sides of buildings, on posters pasted everywhere. I saw young Portuguese marching with the Red flag, with its emblems of the five-pointed star, the hammer, the sickle. The closer I came to Fatima, the more Communist symbols I saw displayed. Pilgrims that year were told to stay away from the Cova da Iria. Little wonder, for the message of Fatima includes a warning against the evils of Communism. The "errors of

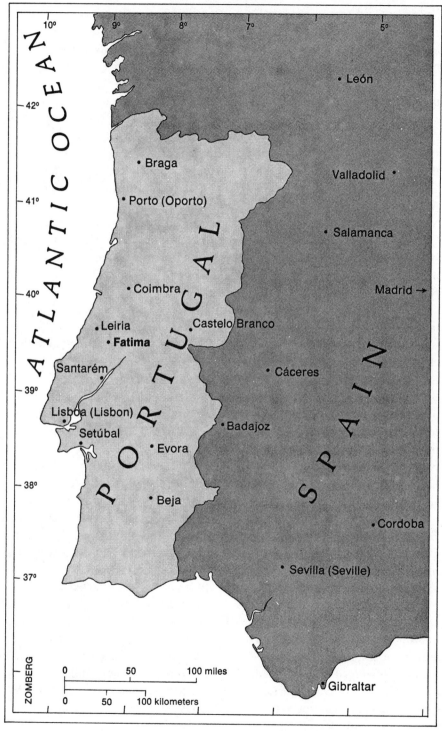

Russia" would spread throughout the world if the requests of the heavenly
Lady were not heeded. I arrived on October 12 and was told that a rumor had
been spread throughout Portugal, that pilgrims were to stay away from Fatima
because the Cova would be bombed on the 13th.

As our pilgrim group approached Fatima, after the 90-mile trek from Lisbon, armed soldiers stopped our buses on the outskirts of the village and
searched them. During religious services in Fatima on the 13th, military planes
circled over the Cova. A military helicopter came to a landing near the entrance
to the Cova. No bombs exploded, and none were found. Later I saw some of
the soldiers making their way through the Cova on their knees, in penance.

Eleven governments were formed, and fell, within the next five years; and
whereas many thought the Communist Party would gain firm control of the
total government, the people of Portugal instead intensified their devotion to
Our Lady of Fatima and came in ever larger numbers to the Cova da Iria in a
spirit of prayer and sacrifice. The peasant farmers in one village, with pitchforks
in hand, met Communist Party leaders, saying, "We'd rather be dead than
Red."

In 1917, Our Lady of Fatima had promised: "In Portugal the dogma of
faith will always be preserved." Some Americans had migrated to Portugal
when they saw modernist heresies seeping into the religious instruction of their
children. Remembering our Lady's promise to preserve the faith in Portugal,
they thought they could escape the enemies of their faith. When in 1974-75
the atheistic Communists, supported by Moscow, gained control of many departments of Portuguese government, many of these same Americans fled Portugal. Their faith in our Lady's promise was weak. She had indeed promised
that the faith would be preserved in Portugal; but she did not say it would be
preserved without a cross. Penance and reparation are essential elements of
Catholic faith. Those who had come to Portugal to avoid a cross in "Our
Lady's Land" fled when the cross appeared.

The Communists offered money to transport people in buses to their rallies.
But their crowds were small. At the same time, much to the frustration of the
Communists, hundreds of thousands of Portuguese pilgrims walked as far as a
hundred and fifty miles, sleeping outdoors in the cold, deprived of conven-
iences, in order to reach the Cova, where there were no material handouts.

People said of the Communist gains and threat of takeover: "It will never
happen here." Dominic dos Rosarios, riding with me on a bus from Fatima to
Lourdes (he was on his way to work in France), told me his father was a witness to the miracle of the sun in 1917. We spoke of the danger that the Communists posed for Portugal. I said, "People of other lands now under Communist governments have also said, 'It will never happen here,' but it did." He responded, "No, it will not happen. The people will never stand for it. Not the
Portuguese people."

I felt sorry to see such a young man—not more than 18 or 19 years of age—leaving Fatima, his native town, and the beautiful land of Portugal to work elsewhere. I was to learn that northern Portugal has many more people than jobs. Thousands of Portuguese emigrate to the more industrialized countries—West Germany, Switzerland, and especially France—where they take unskilled jobs, having in mind to return one day to their native land to retire. Today Paris has the third largest number of Portuguese-born residents (half a million); only metropolitan Lisbon and Porto, each with a population of more than a million, have a larger number.

Antonio Salazar came to power in 1932 in Portugal, and for 36 years he ruled the country as dictator. A stroke disabled him in 1968, and he was succeeded by Marcello Caetano. But on April 25, 1974, a group of army officers overthrew the Caetano regime. They declared Portugal a republic. Since that "April 25 Revolution," there have been several different governments, one of them controlled by the Communists in many departments.

On July 27, 1974, Portugal abandoned its claims to its overseas possessions. The African colonies of Angola and Mozambique and several smaller possessions were granted independence within a year. Only Madeira, the Azores, and the small outpost of Macao near Hong Kong remained under Portuguese control. This action diminished the land holdings of Portugal by 95 percent and its world population by 65 percent. When I returned to Portugal in 1975, I noticed an increase in its black population. Portugal was suddenly faced with having to make provisions for the half-million refugees from its former colonies who found it unsafe to remain in them. Tourism fell off during the 1974-78 period, putting a further damper on the nation's economy. But the refugees, being in large part enterprising people who had left Portugal to venture new careers in the colonies, soon dispersed themselves throughout the country and applied their talents to Portugal's economic development.

According to Sister Lucia, Portugal was spared during World War II because its bishops had consecrated their country to the Immaculate Heart of Mary. When there was a fear of a Communist takeover in 1975, the bishops of Portugal renewed their consecration on May 13, 1975. The Cardinal-Patriarch of Lisbon considered that the Communists' losing control in Portugal subsequently was the result of the people's prayers and penance. At the eighth Fatima Congress at Kevelaer, Germany, on Sept. 17, 1977, he said:

"I can say that it was the consecration made in Fatima to the Immaculate Heart of Mary by the Portuguese bishops in 1931 and 1938 that defended Portugal from the common peril, then so close to its borders. It was the same consecration, renewed in 1940, that saved Portugal from the horrors of the Second World War. . . . And certainly, it was the great devotion of the Portuguese people to the Virgin Mary, ratified anew by the consecration effected by the bishops on May 13, 1975, which halted the advance of Communism among us, when it had already seized control of many departments of our government and threatened to submerge the whole of the public and private life of the Portuguese people."

Communists once boasted that one day they would make Lisbon a headquarters of Communism for taking over nations of the West.

The Communist attempt at world domination started in Russia in 1917. From April to November of that year, when Lenin was busy taking over the Russian government, the Mother of God was appearing to three unlettered and innocent children in the Cova da Iria, in the parish of Fatima, telling the world through them how to prevent "the errors of Russia" from spreading throughout all the nations of the world.

In 1980, less than 40 percent of the world's population resided in free countries. What.has been happening is exactly what the Lady of Fatima had predicted what would happen if people ignored her requests to turn to her Son in daily prayer and Eucharistic reparation.

Some say the small farmers and winegrowers of northern Portugal chiefly saved the country from a Communist takeover in 1975. If Portugal had fallen under Communist rule, it was widely feared, all of Europe would eventually fall to the same evil. The Communists already controlled most of southern Portugal, where the estates had been broken up by Communist influence. The Portuguese Communist Party had won support in some industrial cities and in the working area of Lisbon. But the Communists could not take over Portugal without winning the north, which has almost half of Portugal's population, and which is strongly Catholic. Yet the battle continues. Evil hides in the dark, awaiting its opportunity.

Our Lady of Fatima predicted that the world would be punished "for its crimes by means of war, hunger, and persecution of the Church and the Holy Father. . . . The good will be martyred, the Holy Father will have much to suffer, and various nations will be annihilated. But in the end, my Immaculate Heart will triumph." This last promise of the triumph of the Immaculate Heart is contingent: certain conditions must be met before it can be fulfilled.

II. *The Lady and Her Messages*

The "Age of Mary," as ours is frequently called, may be said to have begun in the middle of the 19th century, with the Church's definition of the dogma concerning Mary's Immaculate Conception (Pius XI, 1854). The dogma of Mary's bodily assumption into heaven was proclaimed by Pius XII in 1950. There has been a succession of Church-approved apparitions of our Lady in this age of Mary.

i

Centuries earlier, in 1531, Mary had appeared four times to Juan Diego, a 57-year-old Indian, near Mexico City. The significance of those apparitions of "Our Lady of Guadalupe" is more fully appreciated in our own times, for it has been discovered that the miraculous, life-size image of herself that our Lady left on the mantle of Juan Diego, on Tepeyac Hill, was in fact also a "letter" from heaven, one that was clearly "read" by the pagan people of Mexico, leading to their conversion—at least eight million of them in seven years—to faith in Jesus Christ. (The portrait of Our Lady of Guadalupe is often compared, for its ability to awaken faith, with the Holy Shroud of Turin.)

The Indian people of Mexico recognized almost immediately, what has taken the rest of the world until now to recognize, that there are hieroglyphics (picture-writing) included in the miraculous portrait of Our Lady of Guadalupe.

Our Lady told Juan Diego to inform Bishop Zumarraga of Mexico City that a temple should be built on Tepeyac Hill. She caused a bouquet of Castilian roses—which did not grow in Mexico but were to be found only in Spain—to appear in Juan's *tilma* (cloak). When Juan took the roses to the bishop and let them fall from his *tilma* to the floor, there appeared on the *tilma* the image of the Virgin, which is today enshrined in the Basilica of Our Lady of Guadalupe, on Tepeyac Hill.

Our Lady had spoken to Juan in Nahautl, his native language—spoken as a second language in central Mexico to the present day. Our Lady appeared also to Juan Diego's uncle, Juan Bernardine, whom she miraculously cured; and in speaking to him she used the Nahautl phrase "te coatlaxopeuh." When he reported the Lady's message to Spanish-speaking persons, they heard what sounded like "Guadalupe," a familiar place-name. But scholars now know that what our lady said to the uncle was: "Her precious image will be thus known [by the name of] the entirely perfect virgin, holy Mary, and it will crush, stamp out, or eradicate [the religion of] the stone serpent." (*Te* means "stone," *coa* means "serpent," *tla* is the noun-ending and can be translated "the," and *xopeuh* means "crush" or "stamp out.")

The significance of this message has much to do with the "stone serpent." This "serpent" was a comet that had appeared at intervals for more than a thousand years and looked like a terrible serpent of fire. When it came close to earth, it caused panic; and the native Mexicans had worshiped it since ancient times. They named it *quetzalcoatl*—the Serpent with Feathers, or the flying serpent. The likeness of this pagan god, carved out of stone, can be seen in ancient pyramids in Mexico. In the image of Our Lady of Guadalupe, the black, burned-out crescent on which the Virgin stands is recognized to be the dead comet. The "message" to the pagan Mexicans was that *Quetzalcoatl*, the god they had been worshiping, the crooked serpent that flew through space, was now dead.

The true God, the invisible God, was "written into" what others had seen as only a beautiful picture.

The Mexicans had offered human sacrifices to such gods as the serpent-comet and the sun. On the Guadalupe image, the Virgin stands *in front of* the sun, blotting it out, while its rays are visible surrounding her. Juan Diego and his contemporaries understood the meaning: The Lady was greater than the sun, and the sun was no god. They had also worshiped stars; the Lady's blue mantle, covered with stars, told them that the invisible, true God made the stars. The black cross on the brooch at the neck of the Lady's tunic reminded the Mexicans of the cross that they had seen the Spaniards venerating. When the Mexicans asked Juan Diego the meaning of the cross, he told them that the true God, who was invisible, had become man; that His name was Jesus Christ, and that He had died on a cross for them, offering His life to God the Father.

The 20,000 bloody human sacrifices that the pagan Mexicans had been offering to a false god each year came to an end, as the Indians turned to Jesus in the Holy Eucharist, the unbloody renewal of His sacrifice on the cross.

In 1962, 431 years after our Lady gave a portrait image of herself to the pagan people of Mexico, with a hieroglyphic message, there was discovered, through greatly enlarged photographs of the eyes of the image, the images of three persons in the pupil of the eye. The entire image of the Virgin, artists and scientists claim, could not possibly have been painted on such rough cactus-fiber material as that of Juan Diego's *tilma*—yet the image is there. There is no trace of paint-brush marks, and it has been found impossible to mix paints and come up with exactly the same hues visible on the image. The scientifically unexplainable portrait has been found to contain the even harder-to-account-for images of three persons in the pupil of the eye. One of the images is thought to be of Juan Diego himself, and the others are apparently of those who were present the moment Juan Diego let his *tilma* fall open so Bishop Zumarraga could behold the Castilian roses (the "sign" he had secretly prayed for)—the moment when the Mother of God imprinted on the *tilma* the image of herself even as she was beholding the three of them. A further wonder: how does cactus-fiber cloth, with a life-expectancy of about 25 years, hang together for more than 450 years, retaining its brilliantly colored image unfaded? It is an image which has survived an attempted bombing on November 14, 1921, by anti-religious political fanatics, and even nitric acid, which a silversmith accidentally spilled over the cloth when cleaning the frame.

What did the beautiful Lady from heaven say to Juan Diego? "Know and take heed, you, the least of my sons, that I am Holy Mary ever Virgin, Mother of the true God, for whom we live, the Creator of the world, Maker of heaven and earth. I urgently desire that a temple be built to me here, to bear witness to my love, my compassion, my aid and protection. . . . Go to the palace of the Bishop in Mexico and say that I sent you to make manifest to him my great desire. . . ."

Our Lady of Guadalupe holds her hands folded in prayer—as she did also at Fatima 386 years later. At Fatima also, she asked for the building of a chapel. At the final apparition, she again blocked out the sun. "And opening her hands, she made them reflect on the sun," wrote Sister Lucia. "While she ascended, the reflection from her person was projected on the sun itself. That is the reason why I cried aloud, 'Look at the sun.' My intention was not to call the attention of the people to it, because I was not conscious of their presence. I was guided to do so by an interior impulse."

At the time Our Lady of Guadalupe appeared to Juan Diego, the Mexicans, being treated badly, were planning to attack and destroy the Spanish colonists. Bishop Zumarraga, seeing the danger, had secretly asked the Blessed Virgin Mary, to whom he had a special devotion, for a sign that she would help. Our Lady acted as Our Lady of Peace on Tepeyac Hill, in giving the roses and the miraculous picture. So too at Fatima, she came as Our Lady of Light and of Peace. Before the miracle of the sun, she said to the three children at Fatima, "I want to tell you that I wish a chapel to be erected here in my honor, for I am the Lady of the Rosary. Continue to say the Rosary every day. The war [World War I] will soon end, and the soldiers will return to their homes" (Oct. 13, 1917). At Fatima, our Lady also had a star on her robe, just above her feet. At Fatima, an angel appeared to the children three times before Our Lady appeared to them. In the Guadalupe image, an angel is shown at the Lady's feet.

ii

St. Catherine Labouré (canonized in 1947) was a Daughter of Charity of St. Vincent de Paul in Paris. Our Blessed Lady revealed to her, in 1830, a distinctive oval-shaped medal. On one side of the medal is an image of Mary, as

Our Lady of Grace, with hands outstretched and with these words surrounding her: "O Mary conceived without sin, pray for us who have recourse to thee." On the reverse side, there was the letter M with a cross and twelve stars; below the M were the hearts of Jesus and Mary. An angel in the form of a small child led Catherine to the chapel where Our Lady was waiting. The Lady was wearing 15 gold rings. At that time it was popular to use marked rings in place of chained beads for rosaries.

The rings worn by the Lady represented the fifteen mysteries of the Rosary. When our Lady gave her name at Fatima, she called herself the "Lady of the Rosary." She did not use the Portuguese word *terca* (five decades of the Rosary, which, during each of the six apparitions, she asked to be prayed *daily*), but rather *rosario*, meaning all 15 mysteries of the Rosary. Both at Fatima and at Paris, she identified herself with the Rosary and its 15 mysteries.

In 1846, our Blessed Lady appeared in La Salette, in southern France, in the diocese of Grenoble, to two uneducated peasant children who happened to meet each other while grazing their cattle. Mélanie Matthieu, age fifteen, and Maximin Giraud, age eleven, fell asleep one afternoon on the hillside. Waking up, they saw a beautiful Lady sitting on a rock in the bed of a small dried-up stream. She held her hands and was weeping; but she reassured the children and told them each separately what she called "a secret." The secret, to the present day, is only partially revealed. In 1851, the children told Pope Pius IX what the Lady had said to them.

When others would ask about the message, the children would answer that there was need for humility, prayer, and penance; also, that a dire punishment would await the human race if it did not repent. Famine, earthquakes, and epidemics of mortal illness would come upon people. Mélanie revealed part of the secret in 1948, but at the Holy See's request, the children made nothing further of the LaSalette revelation public. It is known that our Lady had complained to the children about the abuse of Sunday, about failures to participate in the Holy Sacrifice of the Mass, and about cursing and similar matters. Devotion to Our Lady of LaSalette was approved by the Bishop of Grenoble in 1851 and by the popes since Pius XI.

iii

In 1858, our Lady appeared eighteen times at the grotto of Massabielle, near Lourdes, France, to a fourteen-year-old peasant girl, Bernadette Soubirous. Our Lady would reveal her Immaculate Heart in 1917 at Fatima; at Lourdes she gave her name in this fashion: "I am the Immaculate Conception."

St. Bernadette described our Lady as brighter than the sun. The Lady blessed herself in the name of the Father and of the Son and of the Holy Spirit. She merely listened as Bernadette prayed the Hail Marys of the Rosary, moving the beads gracefully through her fingers in harmony with the young girl's prayers. Only when Bernadette prayed the "Glory be. . . ." did the Lady join in to praise the Holy Trinity.

Just four years before, Pius XI had defined the dogma of the Immaculate Conception; and now, in 1858, heaven was giving its own testimony to the sinlessness of the ever-virgin Mary, Mother of God. Mary chose the Feast of the Annunciation, March 25, to say to Bernadette, "I am the Immaculate Conception." The Annunciation occurred when "the Word was made flesh and dwelt among us." To enable her to be the worthy mother of the Word of God made flesh, Mary had been kept entirely sinless, immaculate.

Our Lady of Lourdes held her rosary draped over her elbow when she was not following Bernadette in prayer. A miraculous spring appeared when, while a crowd of people watched, Bernadette dug into the floor of the grotto at the Lady's bidding. At first, there was only a trickle of water; but soon it grew into a torrent. To the present day, the spring pours out 27,000 gallons of water a day. As earlier at Tepeyac and later at Fatima, the Lady asked that a chapel be built near the grotto. "Pray and do penance for the conversion of the world," was our Lady's special message at Lourdes.

Miracles of healing began to happen almost immediately at the grotto of Massabielle, especially in connection with bathing in the water or during the solemn blessings with the Holy Eucharist. In 1882, a medical bureau was established to test the authenticity of reported cures. Believers and nonbelievers have made up the medical bureau, with any doctor welcome to take part in the examination of the alleged cures. Up to 500 doctors of all faiths (or of no faith) have taken advantage each year. The bureau's procedures are most exacting, and no miraculous cure is claimed if it can offer any possible natural explanation for an improvement in health.

A church was built above the grotto; and then, beside it, from 1883 to 1901, the magnificent Church of the Rosary was built. So famous did the apparitions of Lourdes become that in 1907 Pope Pius X extended a feast in honor of Our Lady of Lourdes (February 11) to the universal Church.

iv

In 1871, our Lady appeared at Pontmain, 30 miles from Laval, France, in the northwest corner of Province Mayeene. In the Franco-Prussian War of 1870, the German army had taken Paris, and Laval had resigned itself to capture. Then, on the evening of January 17, 1871, at 5:30, Joseph and Eugène Barbedette (age ten and twelve, respectively) witnessed a vision of our Lady in the sky, for several hours. Hearing news of the vision, several others joined Joseph and Eugène. A teaching Sister from a nearby convent brought with her some children; they could see the Lady, but she could not. Babies clapped their hands when they saw the vision; their mothers saw nothing. At the suggestion of the parish priest, all knelt in prayer. The Lady, smiling, unrolled a scroll near her feet. The children read the words: "Pray, children. God will hear you. My Son allows Himself to be moved by compassion."

The next day, it was learned that the German army had withdrawn during the period when the vision occurred. Miracles followed the apparition, giving credence to its authenticity. Today a large basilica-shrine to Our Lady of Hope marks the place of the vision. A statue of the Lady was sculptured according to the description of the children; they reported that the Lady's image grew in size as they prayed the Rosary with her.

v

In 1879, an unusual Marian apparition was reported at Knock, Co. Mayo, Ireland. The district lay in the center of a region that was suffering general distress because of famines and other hardships. It had rained all day in the quiet village of Knock, on August 21. The wind and rain continued unabated in the evening when Margaret Beirne went to lock up the parish church for the night. She noticed an unusual brightness over the church but paid little attention to it. A little later, others coming in view of the church gable thought at first they saw statues in front of the gable wall. Then they noticed that the figures were moving. At least fifteen persons, including Margaret, saw the vision, which formed a sort of tableau:

The Blessed Virgin, clothed in white garments, was wearing a large, brilliant crown. Her hands were raised as if in prayer; her eyes were turned heavenward. On her right was St. Joseph, with head inclined toward Mary. At her left stood St. John the Evangelist, vested as a bishop, holding a book in his right hand, raised as if he were preaching. To the left of St. John was an altar on which stood a cross and a young lamb ("about eight weeks old"), around which hovered wings of angels. The background gable wall was bathed in a cloud of light.

The vision lasted for two hours. Even though rain continued to fall heavily, the figures and the area where they stood remained entirely dry. Witnesses heard no word spoken. There was no oral message. The *religious* meaning of the vision includes: our Lady as universal mediatrix; St. Joseph as spouse to Mary and protector of the Church; St. John, "the disciple whom Jesus loved," as model of bishops and priests, as representative of the human race on Mt. Calvary in receiving Mary as our Mother, as authoritative teacher, and as a sign of episcopal power and the unbroken line of apostolic succession in the Catholic Church; and the lamb as Christ, who takes away the sins of the world through His sacrifice on the cross, a sacrifice perpetuated at Mass.

The apparition at Knock may be interpreted as a heavenly appeal to live the full Catholic life, firm in faith, in a time when the spirit of atheism is more and more overtaking the world. The Catholic people of Ireland believe that their devotion to the Rosary has merited for them the grace of perseverance in the faith.

vi

The Marian apparitions at Fatima in 1917 took place just short of four decades following the apparition at Knock. At Fatima, our Lady said, "I am the Lady of the Rosary." The revelations and circumstances surrounding the Fatima apparitions indicate that our Lady promised her special care of everyone who prays the Rosary regularly. Only at Fatima did she identify herself as "Lady of the Rosary." I have come to believe that by praying the Rosary properly, our every need will be answered, even the needs of our natural life. Each time the Lady appeared at Fatima, she asked for the daily praying of the Rosary—the *terca*. At Fatima, she revealed the most "complete" and profound of her messages. Yet each apparition has built upon previous ones; and the authenticity of each has been determined on the basis, in part, of its harmony with the Gospels and the beliefs of the Church.

vii

Between November 29, 1932, and January 3, 1933, our Lady appeared to five Belgian children, ranging in age from nine to fifteen, on thirty-three occasions in the small village of Beauraing, in the Vallon district of Belgium. On November 29, the five children, while walking over a railway viaduct, saw the Virgin with arms outstretched, dressed in white, veiled, with a crown of golden rays around her head, and a gold heart on her breast. In a subsequent vision she told the children always to be good.

At first, public processions were forbidden. Ten years of investigation followed; numerous miracles were reported by those who came to the shrine that had been built on the site of the apparitions. On July 2, 1949, Bishop Charue of Namur approved of public devotion to "Our Lady of Beauraing."

At her last appearance to the children, our Lady asked the oldest boy: "Do you love my Son?"

"O yes, my Lady."

"Do you love me?"

"Yes."

"Then sacrifice yourself to me."

viii

At Banneux, near Liège, Belgium, our Lady appeared to Mariette Beco, a poor, eleven-year-old Belgian child, in the garden of her home on January 16, 1933. Our Lady said that she had come to relieve the ills and sufferings of the poor of all nations. Two days later, Mariette's father, an avowed atheist, went with her to the garden; but he saw nothing. Nonetheless, he was instantly converted, overcome with the sense of holiness in the presence of an unseen power.

After years of investigation, the Holy See approved of public devotion to Our Lady of Banneux, under the title of "Our Lady of the Poor." On the wall of the village chapel is a painting of the Lady, made according to Mariette's description. It shows Mary robed in white, with a blue sash around her waist, and with a rosary draped over her right arm.

A loving mother cares for her children; she is solicitous for their needs. The Marian apparitions we have just reviewed show that our heavenly Mother has—in God's providence—broken into our time upon earth with an "explosion of the supernatural" (as her apparitions at Fatima have been described). She is the "Mother of the Church," as Pope Paul VI named her when he spoke to the Council Fathers at the Second Vatican Council.

The peace of the world requires grace in souls dispensed by the one essential Mediator, Christ; but dispensed also *through* the intercession of His Mother—and our Mother. Just as Jesus spoke of the First Person of the Blessed Trinity as "my Father and your Father" (John 20.17), so He might speak of "my Mother and your Mother" ("Behold your mother," John 19.27).

Mary is the greatest woman God ever created. She has a dignity greater than which no merely human creature can be elevated. She is the Immaculate Conception, "tainted nature's solitary boast." To the Woman who came from heaven at Fatima, we can pray: "You are all beautiful, O Mary, and there is no stain of sin in you." She herself had announced, under the inspiration of the Holy Spirit, whose Spouse she is: "My soul magnifies the Lord and my spirit rejoices in God my Savior, because he has regarded the lowliness of his handmaid; for, behold, henceforth all generations shall call me blessed; because he who is mighty has done great things for me, and holy is his name" (Luke 1.46-49).

We glimpse Mary's magnificence in the angel's description of her—"full of grace" (Luke 1:28). Mary, Mother of the Word, Mother of the Redeemer of the human race, was blessed because she surrendered so perfectly to God's will. "Blessed is she who has believed, because the things promised her by the Lord shall be accomplished" (Luke 1.45). So magnificent is her union with the Blessed Trinity—as daughter of God the Father, mother of God the Son, and spouse of the Holy Spirit—that we can scarcely invoke her intercession, or contemplate her beauty and power, without at the same time finding ourselves closer to God. Mary is not a goddess; but from her privilege as the mother of Jesus Christ, the Second Person of the Trinity become man, flows everything else we might rightly say of her.

In the third century, Mary was already commonly addressed under the title *Theotokos*, Mother of God. Origen (*c*.185-*c*.254) gave her that title, as did others. The Council of Ephesus (431) defined it as the belief of the Church—that Mary is properly called the "Mother of God."

The Person whom Mary conceived in her womb had two natures, one divine, the other human. As the Son of God, the Person conceived in her by the power of the Holy Spirit was eternal and proceeded from the First Person of the Blessed Trinity. It was not a *human* person whom she conceived. The angel told her how it would come about: "The Holy Spirit shall come upon thee and the power of the Most High shall overshadow thee; and therefore the Holy One to be born shall be called the Son of God" (Luke 1.35). Through her conceiving the human *nature* of Christ, there took place the *hypostatic union*—the union of the human and divine natures in the one divine Person of Jesus Christ. This union was accomplished at Mary's free consent. That which God first willed, and which was in the intellect and will of God from all eternity ("I have loved you with an everlasting love," Jeremiah 31.3), Mary willed in time.

As Mother of God, Mary has a dignity greater than all the angels and saints collectively. This heavenly Lady, originally of our earth, and Mother still of all human creatures upon earth, can look into the eyes of the God-Man and say, "My son." And He who is both God and Man can look to this loveliest of creatures and say, "My mother." What a privilege that Jesus, who called His Father *our* Father as well (for such we are by adoption through grace), has given His Mother to us as our spiritual Mother through the same grace.

The Church has firmly believed that Mary was herself conceived without original sin; that her soul was never stained by the slightest sin during her life upon earth; that she was "ever-Virgin"—before, during, and after the birth of Jesus Christ, the Word made flesh; and that her body was assumed into heaven.

Pope Pius IX defined the Church's faith in Mary's privileged freedom from original sin in these words: "The most holy Virgin Mary was, in the first moment of her conception, by a unique gift of grace and privilege of almighty God, in view of the merits of Jesus Christ the Redeemer of mankind, preserved free from all stain of original sin." Mary did not merit this privilege; it was a free gift of God, who loved her from all eternity in the counsels of the Blessed Trinity. Similarly, Pope Pius XII declared of her: "Mary, the immaculate perpetually virgin Mother of God, after the completion of her earthly life, was assumed body and soul into the glory of heaven" (1950). Being "full of grace," Mary was preserved from the consequences of sin: corruption of the body after death, and postponement of bodily happiness in heaven.

Belief in Mary's bodily assumption into heaven was passed on to new generations of Christians, beginning in the first Christian century. The "deposit of faith," with its one source (God), comes to us through the channels of Sacred Scripture, the Magisterium (the teaching Church), and Tradition. Pius XII singled out the truth that, as the body of Jesus Christ originated from the body of Mary (*caro Jesu est caro Mariae*), her body was preserved unimpaired in virginal integrity, and therefore it was fitting that it should not be subject to the destruction of the body after death. So closely did Mary share in Christ's redemptive mission while on earth that she rightly joins her Son in His bodily glorification.

Vatican Council II gave its blessing to Mary's title as Mediatrix of Grace in the *Dogmatic Constitution on the Church* (62). "This motherhood of Mary in the order of grace continues uninterruptedly from the consent which she loyally gave at the Annunciation and which she sustained without wavering beneath the cross, until the eternal fulfillment of all the elect. Taken up to heaven she did not lay aside this saving office, but by her manifold intercession continues to bring us the gifts of eternal salvation. By her maternal charity, she cares for the brethren of her Son, who still journey on earth surrounded by dangers and difficulties until they are led into their blessed home. Therefore the Blessed Virgin is invoked in the Church under the titles of Advocate, Helper, Benefactress, and Mediatrix. This, however, is so understood that it neither takes away anything from nor adds anything to the dignity and efficacy of Christ the one Mediator."

The same Council also taught that Mary was "enriched from the first instant of her conception with the splendor of an entirely unique holiness." St. Alphonsus de Liguori and other doctors of the Church have said that her holiness was "of a superior order to that of all other men and angels." Mary can be called the "Sacrament of the Holy Spirit" for she is the greatest sign of the workings of the Holy Spirit. The graces merited by Jesus Christ are given through her intercession. It is of divine providence that, whether the faithful are mindful or not to ask graces through Mary's intercession, nonetheless what grace they receive—since she is a good Mother who knows how to give what her children need, even before they ask—she bestows on behalf of her divine Son, the sole essential Mediator. How greatly it pleases the divine Son to have His brothers and sisters, the members of His Mystical Body, request graces not only from Him but through the intercession of His Mother.

It is not the case that giving such honor to the Mother distracts from the honor due the Son. If I were to praise the mother of a friend, I would be most surprised if the friend were to turn on me and say, "Why do you honor my mother? Don't you know you are taking away from the love and honor you owe me when you do that?" I would think my friend had become deranged. Rather, in honoring Mary, we honor the Son, who said to us, "Behold your mother."

St. Alphonsus Mary de Liguori (1696-1787), who founded the Congregation of the Most Holy Redeemer (or Redemptorists), in his magnificent work *The Glories of Mary*, complained of a certain "modern" writer of his time who was not exactly pleased with the proposition that *all that we receive from our Lord comes through Mary.* Alphonsus wrote: "Although in other respects he speaks of true and false devotion with much learning and piety, yet when he treats of devotion toward the Divine Mother he seems to grudge her that glory which was given her without scruple by a Saint Germanus, a Saint Anselm, a Saint John Damascene, a Saint Bonaventure, a Saint Antonius, a Saint Bernardine, the venerable Abbot of Celles, ... who had no difficulty in affirming that the intercession of Mary is not only useful but necessary. ... We most readily admit that Jesus Christ is the only Mediator of justice, according to the distinction just made, and that by His merits He obtains us all graces and salvation; but we say that Mary is the Mediatress of grace; and that receiving all she obtains through Jesus Christ, and because she prays and asks for it in the name of Jesus Christ, yet all the same whatever graces we receive, they come to us through her intercession."

In a similiar vein, Sister Lucia wrote (by order of her bishop) a report of what the Lady said to her during the May 13, 1917, apparition:

" 'I am from heaven. ... Do you wish to offer up to God all the sufferings He desires to send you in reparation for the sins by which He is offended, and in supplication for the conversion of sinners?' 'Yes, we do.' 'Go, then, for you will have much to suffer, but the grace of God will comfort you.'

"While pronouncing these last words ["the grace of God"], our Lady opened her hands for the first time, shedding on us a light so intense that it seemed as a reflex glancing from her hands and penetrating to the inmost recesses of our hearts, making us see ourselves in God, Who was that Light, more clearly than we could see ourselves in a mirror. . . ."

If the Church were to define another doctrine as a dogma of faith, it might well be that of Mary's role as Mediatrix of grace.

If we consider, in faith, Mary's special place in creation and her role in "the economy of salvation," her message to the world at Fatima becomes more intelligible; and we see that it is fitting that the Mother of the Church should have the role she carried out at Fatima. Her role, as universal intercessor for all her children, is an active one, as she attested both at Lourdes and at Fatima. Her message is not simply for France or Portugal but for the entire world. Her love and care are for individuals, but her Immaculate Heart embraces—as the Mother of the Word-made-flesh and Mother of the Church—all of humanity.

Mary's being chosen to appear with a message for the world, as Mediatrix, as Mother, is consistent with her title of "Mother of the Church." As Pope Paul VI said of her when the *Dogmatic Constitution on the Church* was published: "It is the first time, in fact—and saying it fills our souls with profound emotion—that an Ecumenical Council has presented such a vast synthesis of the Catholic doctrine regarding the place which the Blessed Mary occupies in the mystery of Christ and of the Church. . . . The reality of the Church is not exhausted in its hierarchial structure, in its liturgy, in its sacraments, in its juridical ordinances. The intimate, the primary source of its sanctifying effectiveness is to be sought in its mystic union with Christ; a union which we cannot conceive as separate from her who is the Mother of the Word Incarnate and whom Jesus Christ Himself wanted closely united to Himself for our salvation. Thus the loving contemplation of the marvels worked by God in His Holy Mother must find its proper perspective in the vision of the Church. And knowledge of the true Catholic doctrine concerning Mary will always be a key to the exact understanding of the mystery of Christ and of the Church.

"[Meditating] on these close relationships between Mary and the Church, . . . we have felt it opportune to consecrate . . . a title which was suggested in honor of the Virgin from various parts of the Catholic world and which is particularly dear to us because it sums up in an admirable synthesis the privileged position recognized by the Council for the Virgin in the Holy Church.

"Therefore, for the glory of the Virgin Mary and for our own consolation, we proclaim the Most Blessed Mary Mother of the Church, that is to say, of all the people of God, of the faithful as well as of the pastors, who call her the most loving Mother. And we wish that the Mother of God should be still more honored and invoked by the whole of Christendom through this most sweet title.

"O Virgin Mary, Mother of the Church, to you we commend the entire Church and our Ecumenical Council. . . ."

Pope Paul announced, in the same address, that he would send a Golden Rose to Fatima; and the Council Fathers rose in long applause. A Golden Rose blessed by the pope, and sent as a token of special honor to some notable person or institution, is most commonly given in token of special joy; and in the case of the Golden Rose sent to Fatima, it gave special significance to the Sanctuary there.

A few years afterward, Paul VI went to Fatima himself, on May 13, 1967, the 50th anniversary of the first apparition of our Lady there. "We come here deeply moved and with a tremendous joy in our hearts," he said. "We are a pilgrim to Fatima. We come from Rome to the Cova da Iria with ardent supplications for peace in the Church and in the world."

Pope Paul VI had called Sister Lucia from her cloistered Carmelite monastery in Coimbra to join him in Fatima as a pilgrim. When he, at one important moment before the millions gathered in the Cova, presented her to them with a lovely, simple gesture, the multitude applauded with great enthusiasm.

It has become increasingly clear since Vatican Council II, with its aftermath of unrest and rebellion in the Church, as in the world, that the message of Fatima—the need to pray and do penance for peace—is of worldwide significance. Our Lady of Fatima warned: "If my wishes are fulfilled, Russia will be converted and there will be peace. If not, Russia will spread her errors throughout the world, promoting wars and persecution of the Church" (July 13, 1917). In the early 1980s, there were signs that the world was awakening to the fact that it was truly in battle against the spreading of the "errors" of Russia. In the same message, our Lady spoke of the faith being preserved; and

*Pope Paul VI honored the occasion of the
fiftieth anniversary of the first apparition at Fatima
by going to Fatima as a pilgrim and by calling
Sister Lucia from her monastery in Coimbra to join him.
The Vatican also released three stamps commemorating the occasion.*

eminent theologians have seen in her words the warning that if her wishes were ignored, great suffering would come to the Holy Father and that the faith would be disturbed in many nations.

It is well that we consider why it was that Mary, the Mother of the Church, the Mediatrix of All Grace, the woman of faith of Sacred Scripture, the model of everything the Church is and hopes to become, should have been chosen to give a message for the world in these our times.

The Miraculous Medal and the Knights of the Immaculata

OUR LADY of the Miraculous Medal. The Miraculous Medal was struck at our Lady's own wish, two years after she appeared to St. Catherine Labouré in 1830. It is a symbol and memorial of her most cherished privilege — the Immaculate Conception. She is depicted on

Meditation Prayer
With the Miraculous Medal

Mary, this medal is a sign and a guarantee of your presence. You are present because your power is present, your voice is present and your love is present.

Therefore, O Wonderful Sinless Woman and our mystical mother, we call on you now to fulfill your guarantee. Bring us the great graces you promised to those who carry this medal, especially to those who wear it around their neck. Make us perceive your presence now and always. Make us consciously experience your power, your love and your guidance, that in their strength we may begin to share in your perfect response to God and to each of his creatures, and join in your war with the ancient Serpent.

Help us utterly abandon our self-centered feelings and preoccupations. Help us hear and understand you. Teach us to listen and learn. Help us respond to you today and always, that made one with you we might more fully respond with the rest of the Church to the Father, Son and Holy Spirit, participating in their life and unity.

For further information write:

Knights of the Immaculata

1600 W. Park Ave., Libertyville, IL 60048

#109-26

III. The Apparitions at Fatima

Among the dark years in the history of the people of Europe were 1916 and 1917, when the "major powers" were engaging their citizens in a fratricidal war. The First World War caused the deaths of millions. The Bolshevik Revolution in Russia, in 1917, eventually would bring many other nations under the mantle of atheism, religious persecution, and denial of the spiritual values of the human person. The principles represented by the Bolshevik Revolution, which today we know as Communism, were imposed by force by Russia's new regime.

In 1917, Portugal was in a seemingly hopeless situation, politically, socially, economically, and, we might even add, religiously. There were many evil forces in Portugal unsympathetic to the Church. A succession of governments came to power—and quickly fell, all inadequate to solve the small nation's problems. The Portuguese people lost confidence in their rulers as one government followed another; and revolution was the order of the day. The nation's economy was near bankruptcy. Its relatively small population consisted mostly of humble country folk, honest, hard-working, poor in material things. Political leaders attempted to stir up a hatred among the common people toward their faith by attacking the Church. As early as 1911, Alfonso Costa, Head of State, had approved a law that required total separation of Church and State. "Thanks to this law," he said, "Portugal, within two generations, will have succeeded in completely eliminating Catholicism." Peasant school-children of devout parents were forced to march through the streets carrying banners proclaiming the slogan "Neither God nor Religion."

Portugal dates its independence as a nation back to 1138, the year of its decisive victory over the Moors. The upheaval of 1916-17—the very years when the Angel of Peace and our Lady were appearing in Portugal—was a sign that Portugal was entering a new phase of its existence. At the time, few in Portugal understood that the heavenly visitations taking place in Fatima marked the beginning of a Sanctuary that was soon to become known as the "altar of the world."

The three shepherd children who were chosen to relate the message of God's Mother to the world, were healthy, normal, even ordinary children at the time of the apparitions. Their only concern had been to herd their sheep, enjoy nature, and have fun. "The weak things of the world has God chosen, that he may confound the strong."

Lucia, the oldest of the three, was born on March 22, 1907. Dark in complexion, she was not considered beautiful; but in her personality she was indeed beautiful, and something of a natural leader. She had black eyes, heavy eyebrows, dark hair, and a slightly flattened nose; thick lips, and a wide mouth. Her even temperament and her sweet and lively disposition made Lucia the "leader" among the children of Aljustrel. They loved her as dearly as she loved them.

Francisco, the next in age, was born on June 11, 1908. He was handsome, with a somewhat round face, and a small mouth. He was peaceable by nature; it did not matter to him if he won or lost at games. He used to spend hours playing a shepherd's flute. His intense love for nature led him to attempt feeding sheep's milk to a snake, or nursing an injured bird back to health. Not much given to talking, he never heard our Lady speak but *saw* her after he began praying the Rosary, five or six beads. The Lady told the other two children that Francisco should pray the Rosary in order to see her.

After the first apparition, Francisco was frequently seen saying the Rosary; for when Lucia asked the Lady if Francisco would go to heaven, the answer came: "He will go there too, but he must say many Rosaries first." The fruit of the apparitions for Francisco was to make him into very much of a contemplative who sought to console his God, who was so saddened by human sin.

Jacinta, Francisco's sister, was born March 11, 1910. She was a beautiful child with fine features in a well-rounded face—bright eyes, thin lips, a small chin, and a captivating, lovely expression.

She loved sheep, especially the lambs, and liked to imagine herself as the Good Shepherd of the Gospels. She would often carry a small lamb home. Things of beauty enticed her: the flowers, the stars, the moon (which she called "our Lady's Lamp"). Before the apparitions began, she had a passion for dancing. The sound of Francisco's flute or any other music was enough to set her feet in motion.

Jacinta loved to pray. She was psychologically incapable of telling a lie, even in the smallest matters. At the same time, she had a natural weakness of possessiveness. She tended toward moodiness. She would pout when she did not get her way in games, and sometimes needed to be coaxed into returning to play with others. After the apparitions, she developed a profound spirituality of comprehending devotion to the Immaculate Heart, and the virtues of her life rivaled those of an advanced adult spirituality.

These three—Lucia, Jacinta, and Francisco—developed an intimate spiritual bond among themselves. The story of their closeness as told by Sister Lucia in her memoirs—the sacrifices they performed, the sufferings they were sent—is one of the more profound and touching stories of our time. Little wonder, for their story was deep in significance. These messengers for the Lady were given

The three children to whom the Blessed Virgin Mary appeared in the
Cova da Iria near Fatima, Portugal. Jacinta and Francisco Marto
flank Lucia Santos in this photograph taken shortly after
the July 13, 1917, apparition.

a formula for world peace and for avoiding world disaster. When they revealed the formula, they were not believed.

i

In the history of God's chosen people of Israel, the Lord often sent angels as bearers of news. So too in the history of the Church. In this way, Man would better know the word of God and respond to His will in love. In Sacred Scripture, angels prepare for the coming of the Lord. At Fatima in 1916, the Angel of Peace came three times to the children. He was a forerunner, preparing them for spiritual understanding, so they could accept the special graces our Lady would bring them.

Interestingly, Lucia has mentioned that she and three other companions had been visited by a mysterious angelic apparition in 1915; but then a year later, the angelic visitor chose to appear instead to Lucia and her two cousins. Perhaps the other children did not respond to the offered graces during that first visitation?

When Lucia was allowed by her mother to become a shepherdess, the news spread quickly among the other shepherd chidren; most of them came to offer themselves as her companions. She said yes to everybody and agreed to go to the sierra with them all. The following day, the sierra was covered with the shepherds and their flocks.

Lucia did not feel comfortable shepherding in such a crowd, with so much shouting back and forth; so she chose three girls, Teresa Matias, her sister Maria Rosa, and Maria Justino, to go with her the following day, with their flocks, to the hill named Cabeço. They took their flocks almost to the bridge of the hill. Below them lay a broad grove of olive, oak, ilex, and pine trees, which stretched down into the valley.

At about noon, they had lunch; and then Lucia invited her three companions to pray the Rosary with her. Shortly after beginning the Rosary, they saw in front of them something hanging in the air over the grove of trees. "It was a figure like a statue," writes Lucia, "made of snow that the rays from the sun had turned somewhat transparent." They continued their prayers, not knowing what it was. The figure remained as they prayed and kept their eyes fixed upon it. Upon their completing the Rosary, the figure disappeared.

Lucia decided it wise to tell no one, but her companions shared the news of what they had seen. When her mother inquired of Lucia what she saw, the girl would only say, "I don't know. It looked like somebody wrapped up in a sheet!" Lucia did not know how to explain what she saw. Later, as a nun, she wrote, "I meant to say that I couldn't see his face so I said, 'It was not possible to see eyes or hands on it.'" Her mother, making a gesture of disdain, said, "Silly girl's nonsense!"

Some time later, the four girls went to the same spot with their flocks and the same thing took place again. Later, Jacinta and Francisco were given permission to shepherd; and they joined Lucia, accompanying her in place of the other three girls. Lucia, Francisco, and Jacinta were later to see the same figure coming toward them over the olive trees; the vision was preceded by a strong wind that shook the trees and made the children raise their eyes to see what was going on, for the day had been quiet.

This, considered the first apparition of the Angel of Peace to Lucia and her two cousins, took place in the spring of 1916. (Not knowing how to fix exact dates, Lucia, writing of these events later, could only estimate the time.) On a rocky hillside of the Cabeço, the three shepherds had sought shelter among the rocks, as it was a rainy day. Then, when the sky cleared, they engaged in games until the strong wind caught their attention.

A strange light came toward them from the east. As it drew near, they saw "a young man, about fourteen or fifteen years old, whiter than snow, transparent as crystal when the sun shines through it, and of great beauty" (according to Lucia's *Memoirs*).

As the angel drew very close, he said, "Do not be afraid! I am the Angel of Peace. Pray with me." The angel knelt on the ground, bowed down until his forehead touched the ground, and asked the children to pray with him three times the prayer "My God, I believe, I adore. ...." For some days afterward, the children remained overwhelmed with the sense of the presence of God, which the angel had conveyed to them.

Two months later, still in 1916, while the three children were playing near the well behind Lucia's house, the same angel suddenly appeared to them again. He reminded them of his instruction to pray, as he had given it in his first apparition. He then instructed the children: "Pray! Pray very much!" He told them that the Hearts of Jesus and Mary had designs of mercy for them—thus indicating (even before the appearances of our Lady) that the Hearts of Jesus and Mary are inseparable, something the later apparitions of Mary more directly revealed.

The angel's counsel that the children were to make of everything they did a sacrifice was indelibly impressed upon their minds. From then on, they frequently recited the prayer the angel had taught them at the first apparition. Also, they began to offer many sacrifices to God. The effect of the angelic visitations was beginning to take hold; the children were gradually being prepared spiritually for the coming of Mary, who would bring a profound coming of the Lord.

It was autumn of 1916, and the three shepherds were again on the slopes of the Cabeço, where the angel had appeared the first time. There the angel made his third visitation to them. This time, the children were not playing but were prostrate on the ground, saying the prayer that the angel had taught them, when an extraordinary light shone upon them. Noticing the bright light, they looked up and beheld the angel holding a chalice in his left hand with the host suspended above it. From the host some drops of blood fell into the chalice. Leaving the chalice and the host suspended in the air, the angel prostrated himself beside the shepherds and asked them to say the following prayer:

Most Holy Trinity, Father, Son, and Holy Spirit, I adore you profoundly. I offer you the most precious Body, Blood, Soul, and Divinity of Jesus Christ, present in all the tabernacles of the world, in reparation for the outrages, sacrileges, and indifferences by which He is offended. And through the infinite merits of the Sacred Heart of Jesus and the Immaculate Heart of Mary, I beg the conversion of poor sinners.

The manner of the angel's prostrating himself before the Blessed Sacrament is that of Eastern Rite Catholics and Orthodox Christians of the East. People of Islamic faiths likewise lie prostrate in prayer at various times each day, to Allah, the supreme being of the Muslims. In Mary's taking the name of "Our Lady of *Fatima*," some see evidence of heaven's gradually drawing all the descendants of Adam and those who consider themselves spiritual descendants of the faih of Abraham to unity with Jesus Christ, the Second Adam.

The angel gave Francisco and Jacinta their first Holy Communion by giving them to drink of the contents of the chalice—a manner known to Eastern Christians. Lucia, having already received her First Communion, was given only the sacred host by the angel.

Once the three children had received, the angel again lay prostrate and repeated with them, three times, the same prayer, "Most Holy Trinity. . . ." He then disappeared, having completed his mission.

ii

During the winter months following the third (final) apparition of the angel, the three children continued making sacrifices as the angel had requested, repeating over and over the prayers they had learned from him, with their heads bowed to the ground as they had been taught. The angel had taught them also that by receiving their divine Lord worthily, lovingly, and in faith, in Holy Communion, they could "repair" the crimes of Man and console their God.

Lucia had already made her First Communion, so she was able to receive Communion at Mass in the parish church. But Jacinta and Francisco had to be content with offering to the Most Blessed Trinity the Real Presence of the Lord's Body, Blood, Soul, and Divinity in the tabernacle. They often spent time in the church, in silent adoration, even at times going on their knees about the church as an act of penance. During those winter months, they were going through the final stages of their "preparation." When spring came, the heavens again would open for the Lady who was to bring them a message of peace, love, and salvation—a message from heaven for the world.

May 13, 1917, fell on a Sunday. Under clear skies and beautiful sunshine, the three children went to Mass. Then, carrying their lunches, they led their sheep toward the Cova da Iria, a small semicircular valley about a mile and a half from their homes in Aljustrel.

As they began to play, the children suddenly saw what seemed like a flash of lightning, though the sky was clear and blue. They decided to return home with their flocks, thinking that a sudden rain might be coming. In the mountains and hills of the sierra, sudden showers are often hidden in their approach by the landscape. The children had gone about half-way down the slope, gathering the sheep, when they saw another flash. Taking a few steps farther, they saw before them, over a small holm-oak tree, a Lady, "brighter than the sun," all dressed in white. She radiated a light clearer and more intense than crystal glass filled with sparkling water, when the rays of the burning sun shine through it. The beautiful Lady spoke to the children.

"Do not be afraid. I will do you no harm."

"Where are you from?" asked Lucia.

"I am from heaven."

"What do you want of me?" Lucia asked. (Lucia was the only one of the three children who ever spoke to the Lady during any of the apparitions. Her first question to our Lady in all six apparitions was always, "What do you want of me?")

"I have come to ask you to come here for six months in succession, on the 13th day, at this same hour. Later on, I will tell you who I am and what I want."

The children remained in silence for a time, and then the Lady asked:

"Are you willing to offer yourselves to God and bear all the suffering He wills to send you, as an act of reparation for the sins by which He is offended, and of supplication for the conversion of sinners?"

"Yes, we are willing," Lucia replied for herself and her cousins.

"Then you are going to have much to suffer, but the grace of God will be your comfort. Pray the Rosary every day, in order to obtain peace for the world and the end of the war."

Then (according to Lucia's account), the beautiful Lady from heaven began to rise serenely, going toward the east, until she disappeared in the immensity of space. The brilliant light that surrounded her seemed to open up a path before her in the firmament.

The children remained joyfully spellbound for a time, spending the remainder of the day in the Cova da Iria. As they discussed the apparition, they agreed that they should say nothing to anyone about what happened. Lucia had experienced the trouble caused when, in 1915, her three companions had spread word about the first apparition of the angel. Francisco and Jacinta agreed to keep perfect silence.

But Jacinta had hardly met her parents that evening before she exclaimed,

"Oh, what a beautiful Lady!" and told everything. She was the first to announce the news that was to go around the world—the news that was also to bring humiliation and eventual suffering to the children and to their families. Most people scoffed at the children's reports.

The beautiful Lady had told the children she would return on the 13th of June, at noon. That day was the feast of St. Anthony of Lisbon, the patron saint of Portugal and of the local parish of Fatima; about fifty people accompanied the children to the Cova da Iria. On that occasion, the Lady again appeared to the children, as she had said she would. She told them that Francisco and Jacinta would be taken to heaven soon but that Lucia would stay on earth some time longer. Then she said, "Jesus wishes to make use of you to make me known and loved. He wants to establish in the world devotion to my Immaculate Heart."

"Am I to stay here alone?" Lucia asked sadly.

"No, my daughter. Don't lose heart. I will never forsake you. My Immaculate Heart will be your refuge and the way that will lead you to God." She opened her hands, and in front of the palm of her right hand the children saw a heart encircled by thorns that pierced it. They understood this to signify the Immaculate Heart of Mary, wounded by the sins of humanity, and seeking reparation.

The skepticism of the children's families intensified, as some said it was all the work of the devil.

The following month, on July 13, 1917, the children saw the Lady again—and again only Lucia and Jacinta heard her speak: "Continue to pray the Rosary every day in honor of Our Lady of the Rosary, in order to obtain peace for the world and the end of the war, because only she can help you."

Lucia begged the Lady to perform a miracle so that all could believe.

"In October," came the reply, "I will tell you who I am and what I want, and I will perform a miracle for all to see and believe."

Lucia, filled with joy at the promise of a miracle, then asked the Lady about requests that various persons in need had made to the children—mostly requests for healings and conversions. The Lady answered that it was necessary for the people who had made the requests to pray the Rosary to obtain the special graces they requested. Some would receive their requests, others not.

"Sacrifice yourselves for sinners, and say many times, especially whenever you make some sacrifice: O Jesus, it is for love of you, for the conversion of sinners, and in reparation for the sins committed against the Immaculate Heart of Mary."

This time too, our Lady opened her hands, and a light issuing from them pierced the ground, opening for the children a vision of a sea of fire:

Plunged in this fire were demons and souls that looked like transparent embers, some black or bronze, in human form, driven about by the flames that is-

sued from within themselves, together with clouds of smoke. They were falling on all sides, just as sparks cascade from great fires, without weight or equilibrium, amid cries of pain and despair which horrified us so that we trembled with fear. (It must have been this sight which caused me to cry out, as the people say they heard me exclaim aloud.) The demons could be distinguished by their likeness to terrible, loathsome, and unknown animals, transparent as live coals. Terrified and as if to plead for succour, we raised our eyes to our Lady, who said to us kindly but sadly:

"You have seen hell where the souls of poor sinners go. In order to save them, God wishes to establish in the world devotion to my Immaculate Heart. If you do what I tell you, many souls will be saved, and there will be peace. The war will end, but if people do not cease offending God, another and more terrible war will break out during the pontificate of Pius XI. When you see a night lit up by an unknown light, know that it is the sign God gives you that He is about to punish the world for its crimes by means of war, hunger, and persecution of the Church and the Holy Father. In order to prevent this, I shall come to ask for the consecration of Russia to my Immaculate Heart, and the Communion of reparation on the first Saturdays. If my wishes are fulfilled, Russia will be converted and there will be peace. If not, Russia will spread her errors throughout the world, promoting wars and persecution of the Church. The good will be martyred, the Holy Father will have much to suffer, and various nations will be annihilated. But in the end, my Immaculate Heart will triumph. The Holy Father will consecrate Russia to me and it will be converted, and a time of peace will be conceded to the world. In Portugal the Dogma of Faith will always be preserved. . . . Do not tell this to anybody. You may tell it to Francisco.

When you recite the Rosary, after each mystery say: "O my Jesus, forgive us, save us from the fire of hell, lead all souls to heaven, especially those who are most in need."

A short silence followed, during which our Blessed Lady remained standing above the holm-oak tree and the children beheld her in contemplation. Finally Lucia said:

"Is there anything more that you want of me?"

"No, I do not want anything more of you today."

The Lady then began to rise and move toward the east; as in the previous apparitions, she seemed to disappear into the infinity of space.

The newspapers of Portugal at this time began to take notice of the reported apparitions in Fatima. Some journalists accused the civil authorities of negligence and inefficiency in not putting an end to the "farce" in the Cova da Iria. The administrator of Vila Nova de Ourém, a proud and ambitious man, took the accusations as aimed at himself and decided to take action.

On the morning of August 13, the administrator went to the homes of the children, pretended he had been converted to believing in the apparitions, and invited the three little shepherds to ride with him to the Cova in his carriage. Instead, he took them by a different road to the Town Hall at Vila Nova de Ourém. The children were placed under severe questioning. They were threatened with being thrown into a cauldron of boiling oil if they did not deny the stories they had told about a Lady from heaven appearing in the Cova da Iria.

Each child was interrogated separately; each thought the others had been boiled in oil; but each refused to deny that a Lady from heaven was in fact giving them messages.

The children were not returned to their homes until August 15th. On the 13th, our Lady kept her appointment in the Cova. The now large crowd that had gathered did witness unusual phenomena around noontime but did not see the Lady. They were convinced that she did in fact come but that she soon left because the children were not present. The Lady told the children later that the miracle promised for October 13th would not be as spectacular as it might have been, because the administrator had kept them from keeping their August 13 appointment.

Shortly after they were released from the prison in Ourém, the three children experienced an apparition at a place called Valinhos, very close to Aljustrel. On the occasion, Lucia and Francisco were accompanied by the latter's brother John. Sensing that the Lady was coming—because the sun's brightness dimmed and the air grew suddenly cooler as during previous apparitions—Lucia gave John two coins and asked him to go fetch Jacinta.

As soon as Jacinta joined Lucia and Francisco, our Lady appeared before them, again standing above a holm-oak tree. She repeated her promise to perform a miracle in October "so that all may believe." She asked also for a chapel to be built in the Cova da Iria and for two litters to be made. (It was evident to the children that the litters were to be used to carry images of our Lady in procession.) Jacinta was to carry one litter together with Lucia and two other girls. Francisco was to carry the other with three other boys. "The money placed on the litters is for the feast of Our lady of the Rosary, and what is left over is to help toward the building of a chapel."

At this August apparition, Lucia asked her usual leading question, "What do you want of me?"

"I want you to continue going to the Cova da Iria on the 13th, and to continue saying the Rosary every day. In the last month [October] I will perform a miracle so that all will believe."

To Lucia's request, "I wish to ask you to cure some sick persons," the Lady replied: "Yes, I will cure some of them during the year."

And then with a sad expression the Lady said: "Pray, pray very much and make sacrifices for sinners, for many souls go to hell because they have nobody to pray and make sacrifices for them."

As usual, the Lady left the children by ascending toward the east.

iii

The number of those believing in the apparitions continued to grow, even though every effort was made by civil authorities to put an end to the "farce" of the Cova da Iria.

On September 13th, approximately 25,000 people were present in the Cova at noon. The apparition was in most respects similar to those that preceded:

"What do you want of me?" Lucia asked.

"Continue to pray the Rosary in order to obtain the end of the war. . . . In October, I will perform a miracle so that all may believe."

Our Lady also said: "In October, our Lord will come, and also Our Lady of Sorrows and Our Lady of Carmel. Saint Joseph will appear with the Child Jesus to bless the world. God is pleased with your sacrifices, but He does not want you to sleep with the [penitential] cord on, only to wear it during the daytime."

At Lourdes, according to St. Bernadette, "it seemed all our Lady did was smile." At Fatima, the Lady smiled only once, and that was in September when she said, "God is pleased with your sacrifices."

When Lucia asked for the cure of some sick people, of a deaf-mute and so on, the answer came, "Yes, I will cure some, but not others."

After again promising to perform the miracle in October, our Lady ascended as usual toward the east and disappeared.

When the long-awaited day for the promised miracle arrived, 70,000 to 100,000 people were present in the Cova da Iria. Among them were the devout, the curious, unbelievers, atheists, and also journalists who were there to "unmask the hoax." It had been raining since the evening before; dark, heavy clouds hung over Fatima. The people standing in the Cova were soaked. The rain continued to pour down until the moment of the apparition.

Lucia's mother had decided she had better accompany her daughter this time, for she feared for her child's life. With tears running down her cheeks, she walked beside Lucia saying, "If my daugher is going to die, I want to die at her side." If no miracle took place—Lucia's mother did not believe Lucia was telling the truth—she thought the crowd would turn in anger against her daughter.

When it was exactly noon (according to true sun-time; Portugal was then on "war time"), the Lady arrived. Lucia cried out: "Silence! Be quiet! Our lady is coming!" From that moment on, the three children were unconscious of anything happening around them except the apparition.

"What do you want of me?"

"I want to tell you that a chapel is to be built here in my honor. . . . I am the Lady of the Rosary. Continue always to pray the Rosary every day. The war is going to end."

When Lucia presented petitions on behalf of many others, she again received the answer: "Some yes, but not others. They must amend their lives and ask forgiveness for their sins."

Looking very sad—the sorrowful look and sad tone of voice have remained vivid in Lucia's memory to the present day—the Lady of the Rosary added: "Do not offend the Lord our God any more, because He is already so much offended."

The Mother of God next manifested herself as "brighter than the sun." She opened her hands and made them reflect on the sun. As she ascended, the reflection of the light emanating from her own body continued to be projected on the sun itself In other words, our Lady shone more brightly than the sun.

The little shepherds then beheld, near the sun, the other promised visions. Joseph appeared with the Child Jesus blessing the world, and with Our Lady robed in white with a blue mantle. Joseph and the Child Jesus made the Sign of the Cross with their hands. This vision vanished. Next they saw our Lord and our Lady (who appeared in aspect to be Our Lady of Sorrows). Our Lord (as a man) seemed to bless the world in the same manner as St. Joseph had. Next came an apparition of our Lady under the aspect of Our Lady of Mount Carmel, holding the brown scapular down to the world, indicating (as Lucia later interpreted the gesture) that she still desired people to wear it as a sign of their consecration to the Immaculate Heart of Mary.

At the point where our Lady made herself reflect on the sun, Lucia cried out, "Look at the sun!" The people present took it as an indication of the beginning of the miracle of the sun. Avelino de Almeda, who had been assigned as a special reporter for the anticlerical daily *O Seculo*, wrote the following report for his paper: "The sun looked like a plaque of dull silver, and it was possible to look at it without the least discomfort. It neither burned nor blinded the eyes. It might have been an eclipse which was taking place. But at that moment a great shout went up, and one could hear the spectators nearest at hand shouting: 'A miracle! A miracle! A marvel! A marvel!' "

The clouds had suddenly swung back as the rain stopped. The people stood bareheaded and pallid with fear, searching the sky as the sun "trembled" and made quick, incredible movements outside all cosmic laws. A typical discription was: "The sun danced."

Ti Marto, father of the two younger children, described it this way: "All eyes were fixed on the sky when, at a certain moment, the sun seemed to stop, and then began to move and dance. It stood still, then began to dance once more, until it seemed that it was being detached from the sky and was falling upon us. It was a terrible moment!"

Some of those present, thinking the end of the world had come, prayed aloud for forgiveness of their sins. Some exclaimed, "O Jesus! We are all going to die! ... Our Lady, help us!"

*Following the "miracle of the sun" that occurred during
the October 13, 1917, apparition, many newspapers printed articles
and photographs documenting the event.*

When the sun finally returned to its orbit and stood still, those thousands of people who had been soaked by the rain just minutes before were now completely dry.

When in the May 13, 1917, apparition the Lady had asked the children to come to the Cova da Iria for six successive months, on the 13th day at the same hour, she had added, "And I will return here yet a seventh time." Some people go to Fatima on the anniversaries of the apparitions, hoping to witness our Lady make her seventh appearance. Some students of our Lady's apparitions at Fatima maintain that she has already appeared the seventh time in the Cova, to Lucia alone, before Lucia left for the convent in Porto.

iv

After the apparitions, Francisco was convinced that our Lady would come for him very soon. He lost interest in attending school. Commonly, when he was walking to school with Lucia, who had been *told* by our Lady to learn to read (something seldom accomplished for girls in Portugal at that time), Francisco would say to her: "You go on. I'll go into the church to keep the Hidden Jesus company." He would at times spend the entire day before the Blessed Sacrament, going up to the altar and placing his elbows immediately before the tabernacle. Many people claimed to have received special graces after asking Francisco to pray for them.

In October of 1918, one year after the apparitions, Francisco fell sick. When family members tried to assure him he would get better, he replied, "It is no use. Our Lady wants me in heaven with her."

Francisco, preoccupied with consoling God because of the offenses committed against Him, continued to offer his sufferings up to console Jesus as his illness grew worse. "I am suffering much," he said to Lucia, "but never mind. I suffer everything for love of Jesus and our Lady. I would like to suffer more, but I am unable to do so."

At one point in his illness, he said to his mother, "I no longer have the strength to say the Rosary out loud. When I try to pray the Hail Mary, I can't keep my mind on it any more." This difficulty was another suffering to offer up, for Francisco had prayed the Rosary at every available minute that he could after the beautiful Lady had told him he would go to heaven but that he first must pray many Rosaries.

Francisco said to the parish priest, "Father, I desire to receive Jesus in Holy Communion before I die!" Preparing himself for confession, he called for Lucia and Jacinta and asked them to help him to examine his conscience and to recall any sins he had committed. When they told him of some minor faults, Francisco burst into tears, saying: "I have already confessed those sins, but I'll do so again. Maybe it is because of these sins which I committed that Jesus is so sad! Would you also ask our Lord to forgive me my sins?"

When the priest came, Francisco received Holy Communion for the last time (the only other time being the Communion given him by the angel). In a weakened condition, he asked Jacinta and Lucia to pray the Rosary aloud while he followed their prayers in his heart.

Early on the morning of April 4, 1919, with the sun shining brightly into his small, plain bedroom, Francisco beheld another light, besides the sunlight. "Look, Mother, do you see that beautiful light over there by the door?" The beautiful Lady had evidently come to take him to heaven. He died at ten o'clock that morning.

Francisco's body was buried in a simple grave in the cemetery of St. Anthony's Parish in Fatima. On March 12, 1952, his mortal remains were located and identified with some difficulty. The coffin contained some bones, a bit of hair, and his rosary. The remains were reinterred in the side-chapel on the right-hand side of the high altar in the Basilica of Our Lady of the Rosary.

v

Jacinta, who was only six at the time of the apparitions of the Angel and seven during those of our Lady, saw and heard everything. She never spoke to the angel or to our Lady. The words of our Lady that impressed her deeply were: "The Lord our God is already so much offended" and "Pray very much, and make sacrifices for sinners." The vision of hell had the deepest effect on her. Discovering who the Holy Father was from two priests who had come to Fatima to visit, Jacinta developed a profound love for the Pope, the Vicar of Christ on earth, who would have so much to suffer. Jacinta would say, "Poor Holy Father." Her young mind could not understand why the Pope did not come to Fatima to visit, because everyone else seemed to be coming.

Further sayings of Jacinta, based on communications she said she received when our Lady appeared to her in the Lisbon hospital, include: "God does not wish the death of sinners. He wants them to be converted to give glory to God on earth and in heaven. . . . Our Lady likes those who mortify their senses, and those who help one another to have faith, hope, and charity. . . . If the Government would leave the Church in peace and give liberty to religion, it would have God's blessing. . . . The world is perishing because the people do not meditate. . . . Penance is necessary. If people amend their lives, our Lord will even yet save the world; but if not, punishment will come."

Jacinta's predictions about the manner of her death came to pass. She died *alone* at the exact hour she predicted, at ten-thirty in the evening, February 20, 1920. She was seen resting well shortly before her death, our Lady having removed her pains. Shortly after ten-thirty, she was found dead. Lucia wrote:

What made the biggest impression on Jacinta was the idea of eternity. Even in the middle of a game, she would stop and ask: "But listen! Doesn't hell end

*after many, many years, then? . . . Those people burning in hell, don't they
ever die? And don't they turn into ashes? And if people pray very much for
sinners, won't our Lord get them out of there? And if they make sacrifices as
well? . . . Poor sinners! We have to pray and make many sacrifices for them!"*

Then she went on:

"How good that Lady is! She has already promised to take us to heaven."

Jacinta took this matter of making sacrifices for the conversion of sinners so
much to heart, that she never let a single opportunity escape her. . . . *Every
time she offered her sacrifices to Jesus, she added: "And for the Holy Father."
At the end of the Rosary, she always said three Hail Marys for the Holy Father. . . .*

The day came for Jacinta [who was suffering from tuberculosis] to go to the
hospital. There indeed she was to suffer a great deal. When her mother went to
see her, she asked if she wanted anything. She told her that she wanted to see
me [Lucia]. . . . As soon as Jacinta saw me, she joyfully threw her arms
around me, and asked her mother to leave me with her while she went to do
her shopping. Then I asked her if she was suffering a lot.

*"Yes, I am. But I offer everything for sinners, and in reparation to the Im-
maculate Heart of Mary."* Then, filled with enthusiasm, she spoke of our Lord
and our Lady: *"Oh, how much I love to suffer for love of them, just to give
them pleasure! They greatly love those who suffer for the conversion of sinners."* . . .

Once again, the Blessed Virgin deigned to visit Jacinta, to tell her of new
crosses and sacrifices awaiting her. She gave me the news saying: *"She told me
that I am going to Lisbon to another hospital; that I will not see you again, nor
my parents either, and after suffering a great deal, I shall die alone. But she
said I must not be afraid, since she herself is coming to take me to heaven."*

She hugged me and wept: *"I will never see you again! You won't be coming to visit me there. Oh, please, pray hard for me, because I am going to die
alone!"*

Jacinta suffered terribly right up until the day of her departure for Lisbon.
She kept clinging to me and sobbing. *"I'll never see you again! Nor my mother, nor my brothers, nor my father! I'll never see anybody ever again! And
then, I'll die all alone!"*

At times, she kissed and embraced a crucifix, exclaiming: *"O my Jesus! I
love you, and I want to suffer very much for love of you."* How often did she
say: *"O Jesus! Now you can convert many sinners, because this is really a big
sacrifice!"*

From time to time, she asked me: *"Am I going to die without receiving the
Hidden Jesus [the children's term for the Real Presence of Jesus under the sac-
ramental species of Holy Communion]? If only our Lady would bring Him to
me, when she comes to fetch me!"*

One day I asked her: "What are you going to do in heaven?"

"I'm going to love Jesus very much, and the Immaculate Heart of Mary too. I'm going to pray a lot for you, for sinners, for the Holy Father, for my parents and my brothers and sisters, and for all the people who have asked me to pray for them. . . ."   Lucia's *Memoirs*

The tuberculosis inexorably consumed her small, emaciated body, as she suffered intensely for our Lord.

On one occasion, Jacinta promised to pray much in heaven for priests. She had a profound respect for the priesthood, as priests possess the powers of Jesus Christ. She managed, in the Lisbon hospital, to receive Holy Communion. According to Lucia, of the three children, Jacinta was especially touched by grace and by an understanding knowledge of God, of virtue, and of the meaning of devotion to the Immaculate Heart of Mary. It was only Jacinta who had seen two visions of the Pope deeply suffering on account of the persecutions of the Church, at the well and at the Cabeço.

During the last weeks of her life on earth, Jacinta received many messages from heaven.

Her sayings read more like the wisdom of an adult advanced in spirituality. She pronounced on modesty, the use of food, the custody of the eyes, the will, the use of the tongue. She spoke of avoiding persecutions, greed, lies, envy, and riches. "Our Lord and our Lady are very offended with people because they do not obey the Pope, nor the bishops, nor the priests. . . . Those who rule in the Church are not like other men. Priests should be as the salt of the earth; our Lady is always pleading for them; they should be sincere and pure. Our Lady wants them to be respected as [if they were] her Son. . . . God help those who persecute the Church! . . . Priests must be very, very pure. Priests should concern themselves only with the things of the Church. Disobedience of priests and religious to their superiors displeases our Lord very much."

vi

Lucia's troubles began immediately after the first apparition of Our Lady. While she had been favored by her parents and older brothers and sisters, who called her the "coddler," they now seemed to turn on her, with the exception of her father, who for the most part remained supportive or at least neutral. The villagers joined her family in ridiculing the girl. The parish priest said, "It might be a trick of the devil."

In addition, Lucia had been told by the Lady that Jacinta and Francisco would soon be taken to heaven but that she herself would have to remain on earth, to spread devotion to the Immaculate Heart of God's Mother: "My Immaculate Heart will be your refuge and the way that will lead you to God."

Lucia's own heart was broken with the deaths of Francisco, Jacinta, and then her father, who died in the same epidemic that claimed so many other lives.

In 1921, the Bishop of Leiria-Fatima, José Alves Correia da Silva, arranged that Lucia should leave Aljustrel and be educated by the Dorothean Sisters of Vilar, near Porto in northern Portugal. Lucia left at night for Vilar in utmost secrecy; not even the other girls at the school in Vilar knew of her connection with the Fatima apparitions. Before she left, she bade good-bye to Fatima with a heart full of tears, visiting the well behind her house, where the angel had appeared; Valinhos, where our Lady had appeared in August; the Cabeço, where the children had often played, herding their sheep and picking flowers, and where the angel had given them Holy Communion and taught them Eucharistic reparation; and lastly her beloved Cova da Iria. As the carriage pulled away after midnight, having stopped at the Cova for a final Rosary, Lucia kept looking back, with memories of the events of 1916-17 and the aftermath running through her mind. She left Francisco and Jacinta behind, buried in the Fatima cemetery and in the cemetary of Vila Nova de Ourém, respectively.

Lucia made her profession of vows in the Institute of St. Dorothy in 1928. In 1946, she was asked to make a brief visit to Fatima to identify the exact place of the apparitions. At that time she pointed out the stone on which the angel had stood near the well, as well as the site of his appearance at the Cabeço.

Two years later, in 1948, Lucia received permission to leave the Dorotheans and enter the cloistered Carmelites. Taking the name Sister Maria Lucia of the Immaculate Heart, she entered the Carmel of Coimbra, where she lives to the present day. I have frequently offered Mass there, at St. Theresa's Carmelite Monastery in Coimbra. Contrary to false reports about Lucia that sometimes circulate, she is happy, though she had long been anxious for the consecration of Russia to the Immaculate Heart of Mary by the pope in union with the bishops of the world. That "collegial" consecration finally occurred on May 13, 1982, when Pope John Paul II went to Fatima. Lucia was there to witness it—smiling, according to one report, "as bright as the sun." It was once rumored, also falsely, that Lucia would participate only in the "old" rite of the Mass and rejected the new Order of the Mass approved by Pope Paul VI in 1969.

Sister Lucia has never sought the attention of the world, but rather to avoid it; while our Lord has used her in His own way to spread devotion in the world to the Immaculate Heart of His mother. Nor has she sought a pulpit from which to preach. Hers is a life of prayer and Eucharistic reparation.

On September 12, 1935, when the mortal remains of Jacinta were taken from Vila Nova de Ourém to the cemetery in Fatima, various photographs were taken of her body, which appeared to be incorrupt. Bishop José Alves Correia da Silva sent some of the photographs to Sister Lucia, who at the time resided in the convent of Pontevedra in Spain. On November 17, 1935, Sister Lucia acknowledged receiving the pictures in a letter to him: "Thank you very much for the photographs. I can never express how much I value them, especially those of Jacinta. I felt like removing the wrappings in order to see all of her. . . . I was so enraptured! My joy at seeing the closest friend of my childhood again was so great. . . . She was a child only in years. As to the rest, she already knew how to be virtuous, and to show God and the most holy Virgin her love through sacrifice. . . ."

Canon José Galamba de Oliveria detected from Lucia's response that she had not told all she knew, even though the basic message of our Lady's six appearances at Fatima had been approved by the Church. Canon Galamba encouraged Bishop Alves to get Lucia to tell more. That was why Lucia came to write her *Memoirs*, under religious obedience.

Asking "the most holy Hearts of Jesus and Mary to deign to bless it, and to make use of this act of obedience to obtain the conversion of poor sinners," Lucia wrote the first of four volumes of her *Memoirs* sometime before December 25, 1935, telling all she could remember about Jacinta's life. Even then she was reluctant to include some matters: "In spite of my good will to be obedient," she wrote, "I trust Your Excellency will permit me to withhold certain matters concerning myself as well as Jacinta that I would not wish to be read before I enter eternity. You will not find it strange that I should reserve for eternity certain secrets and other matters. After all, is it not the Blessed Virgin herself who sets me the example? Does not the Holy Gospel tell us that Mary kept all things in her heart? And who better than this Immaculate Heart could have revealed to us the secrets of Divine Mercy? Nonetheless, she kept them to herself as in a garden enclosed, and took them with her to the palace of the Divine King."

Two years after Sister Lucia wrote the first *Memoir*, the Bishop of Leiria-Fatima was convinced that the Fatima events of 1917 had to be studied more deeply; so he ordered Sister Lucia to write the history of her own life and that of the apparitions just as they happened. She consequently wrote her second manuscript between November 7 and 21, 1937.

Four years later, she again complied with a request to write in further detail about Jacinta's life. Completed on August 31, 1941, this is known as the *Third Memoir*.

On October 7, 1941, Bishop Alves ordered Lucia to write everything else she could remember about the miraculous events at Fatima. On December 8, she presented the *Fourth Memoir*.

While the events in the Cova at noon on October 13, 1917, were considered miraculous by thousands present (many self-declared atheists were converted on the spot), yet it did not silence the enemies of religion and of the "supernatural" events the three children of Fatima claimed to have witnessed.

Above: The wooden arch constructed on the site of the apparitions in 1917. Below: The original Capelinha (Chapel of the Apparitions), built in 1918-19 on the site of the apparitions. It was destroyed by dynamite on March 6, 1922, but a new Capelinha was built shortly thereafter.

Ten days afterward, for example, the Masonic Lodge of Santarem drew up a plan to put Catholic devotions and faith to ridicule. Even though the "miracle of the sun" had been witnessed for 32 miles around, it did not impress determined enemies of the faith.

Maria "da Capela" (as she became known), who was one of the early believers in the Fatima apparitions, erected a makeshift shrine in the Cova on the site of the apparitions; it consisted of a wooden arch, a couple of lanterns, some crosses, and so forth. During the night of October 23-24, some individuals from Santarem and from Vila Nova de Ourém went to the Cova da Iria and pirated the site. The newspaper *Diario de Noticias* reported the results: "With an axe they cut the [holm-oak] tree under which [sic] the three shepherd children stood during the famous phenomenon of the 13th of this month, so largely referred to in the press. They took away the tree together with a table on which a modest altar had been arranged and on which a religious image [of the Virgin] had been placed. They also took a wooden arch, two tin lanterns, and two crosses, one made of wood and the other of bamboo cane wrapped in tissue paper."

The plan of the thieves was to use the tree and devotional objects the faithful had placed at its feet to set up an exhibition in the capital and then organize a mock-procession along the main roads of the district. The stolen objects were placed on exhibition in a house near the Santarem seminary. As *Seculo* reported, the procession consisted of two drummers, "while behind came the famous tree on which our Lady had appeared. Next, the wooden arch and the lanterns alight, the table and other objects which the faithful had placed on the improvised altar. To the sound of blasphemous litanies, the procession passed through the principal streets of the city, returning to the Sá da Bandeira Square, where it dispersed."

"The affair was a disgrace," reported the same journalist. "How is it possible that the authorities tolerate such a thing while at the same time they refuse permission for the processions of the Church to which nearly the whole population belongs and whose ceremonies in no way offend the convictions of others?"

The plan of the enemies of Fatima backfired, for the general reaction of Catholics and others who held any sense of decency was one of disgust. Besides, as Maria da Capela said of the occasion: "They thought they had taken the [holm-oak] tree, but they made a mistake and took another."

Lucia herself wrote of the event: "Meanwhile the government did not leave things where they stood. In the place of the apparitions people had put an arch and lanterns which were kept alight. One night some men came in a motorcar to tear down the arch and to cut the tree where the apparitions had taken place. In the morning the news spread rapidly, and I ran to see if it was true. Imagine my joy when I saw that those wretched men had made a mistake and, instead of taking the right tree (which by then was nothing but a small trunk because pilgrims had been taking parts of it for relics), they had cut one of the saplings nearby. I asked our Lady to forgive them, and I prayed for their conversion."

In their satanic effort to destroy any memory of the Fatima events, which they called "Jesuitical inventions," the thieves rather contributed to an unusual increase of faith in the miracle and to a renewal of Catholic faith in the Land of Mary.

José Vale, editor of the newspaper *O Mundo*, made another attempt to discredit the alleged apparitions. In politics he was known as an anarchist; in religion, as an atheist. He produced a series of pamphlets denouncing the apparitions, the priests, and the Jesuits ("who were the customary authors of all ill"). He issued an invitation to "all liberal-minded people" to assemble the following Sunday outside the church in Fatima at the close of its Mass so as to reduce to comedy the events in the Cova da Iria.

The pastor, however, arranged it so that his parishioners were informed that he would offer Mass that Sunday in the Chapel of Our Lady of Ortiga, four miles to the east. An hour before sunrise, the three children set off for Quinta, more than five miles from Fatima, so as to be safe. Those who came to Fatima to ridicule the parishioners found themselves alone.

The sacrilegious theft, the parody in Santarem, and the virulent pamphlets had as their effect to strengthen the minds and hearts of the Portuguese people to accept Fatima, and thus to strengthen their faith. The simple people of the villages in the mountainous countryside were the first to answer the call of the Mother of God. As in the case of Jesus Christ when He was physically upon earth, the poor received the message first. The day after the miracle of the sun, a seemingly endless procession of people could be seen marching toward the Cova da Iria. Then came countless others, until it appeared that all of Portugal was on pilgrimage to the Cova da Iria. Priests heard the confessions of thousands in the open air, long into the night.

Many people came to the Cova to pray for miracles of healing. While such miracles of healing did occur frequently in the early days following the apparitions, especially in connection with the water that sprang up near the Capelinha (the "little chapel" built over the site of the holm-oak tree), miracles of grace, leading to countless conversions, became the chief fruit. A return to the state of grace, a renewal and strengthening of faith in God, and a resolution to prayer and Eucharistic reparation, together with devotion to the Immaculate Heart of Mary—in these ways did "the miracle of Fatima" have its effects.

These demonstrations of faith, and the drawing of souls to the sacraments, especially to the Eucharistic Lord, prompted the bishop of Leiria-Fatima to look favorably on the reports of the supernatural in the Cova da Iria.

IV. 🌳 *Maria dos Anjos and John Marto*

On August 5, 1979—it was a Sunday afternoon—I walked from the Cova area to Aljustrel, to interview Maria dos Anjos, Lucia's sister. She was about to celebrate her eighty-eighth birthday, on August 15.

i

While in Aljustrel, I met Father Joseph Valinho, a Salesian priest and Maria's son. He was home for his mother's birthday.

I showed him some photographs that the papal photographer had taken when I met Pope John Paul II on July 25. During that meeting, I had presented a life-size portrait of Jacinta to his Holiness, who showed great interest in it, asked me about it, and later sent me a letter expressing his appreciation.

Father Valinho, looking through the photographs, mentioned that he was going to visit Lucia in Coimbra on August 10. "How happy Sister Lucia would be to have such a picture." I invited him to choose the best of the photographs and take it with him, on the condition that he also take a letter from me to Sister Lucia. He agreed.

A few days later, when Father Valinho had returned from Coimbra, I asked him what Sister Lucia thought of the picture and the portrait. "She was all smiles," he reported. "She was very happy. She then spoke of the possible canonization of Jacinta." I learned that Sister Lucia had carried the photograph with her throughout the day. (In August 1981, Sister Lucia sent me word that she would love to have a similar portrait painted of Francisco also. I engaged Anita Clause, an artist from Sioux Falls, South Dakota, to paint, in oil colors, a portrait of Francisco holding his rosary; I presented this portrait to Sister Lucia when I went to Coimbra in the summer of 1982.)

I asked Father Valinho if Sister Lucia spoke to him of a chastisement to fall on the world. He replied, "Sister Lucia has always been optimistic. She carries the optimism of the 'triumph of the Immaculate Heart.' The words of Lucia," he said, "have always indicated that Man by his own sin would bring unhappiness and misery upon himself. Such is enough chastisement. Eventually Man will have to realize that he is not finding happiness in this way and will have to turn back to God."

Father Valinho told me of a letter that Sister Lucia had written to him in April 1971. This letter—which I have assisted in circulating to English-speaking friends—reads as follows:

Coimbra, Portugal, April 13, 1971.
Pax Christi.

Dear Father Valinho:

I see from your letter that you are worried about the turmoil and the disorientation of our time. It is indeed sad that so many are allowing themselves to be dominated by the diabolical wave that is enveloping the world, and they are so blind that they cannot see their error. But the principal error is that they have abandoned prayer. Thus they turn away from God, and without God everything is lacking to them. For, "without me you can do nothing" (John xv:5).

What I recommend to you above all is that you get close to the Tabernacle and pray. In fervent prayer you will receive the light, strength, and grace that you need to sustain you, and to share with others.

Guide those under your care with humility, with gentleness, and at the same time with firmness. Because Superiors above all have the duty to maintain the truth in its proper place, always with serenity, with justice and charity. For this reason they need to pray more and more, to keep close to God and to tell Him about all their affairs and all their problems before they discuss them with human beings. Follow this road and you will see that in prayer you will find more science, more light, more strength, more grace and virtue than you could ever achieve by reading many books, or by great studies. Never consider as wasted the time you spend in prayer. You will discover that in prayer God communicates to you the light, strength, and grace you need to do all He expects of you.

The only important thing for us is, to do the will of God; to be where He wants us to be, and to do all He wants of us, but always with humility, knowing that of ourselves we are nothing and that it is God who works in us and through us, to accomplish His work. Therefore, we all need to intensify our life in intimate union with God, and this we can attain only through prayer. It is in prayer that the soul encounters direct contact with God, who is our strength and the source of all Good. Let time be lacking for everything else but never for prayer, and you will accomplish a lot in a short period of time.

Each of us, especially the superior without prayer, or who habitually sacrifices prayer for material things, is like a hollow, split reed that serves only to beat the whites of eggs into castles of foam which without sugar to sustain them soon dissolve and become as polluted water.

For this reason Jesus Christ said, "You are the salt of the earth but if salt loses its strength it is good for nothing but to be thrown out." We can recieve our strength from God alone. We must get close to Him for Him to communi-

cate it to us. We can realize this closeness only through prayer because it is in prayer that the soul encounters direct contact with God.

I would like you to pass on these recommendations to your religious brothers, let them experiment with them, then you can tell me if I was wrong. I am convinced that the principal cause of evil in the world and the falling way of so many consecrated souls is the lack of union with God in prayer. The devil is very smart and watches for our weak points so he can attack us. If we are not careful and attentive in obtaining the strength from God, we will fall because our times are very bad and we are weak. Only God's strength can sustain us.

See that you take everything with calmness and with great confidence in God. He will do for us what we cannot do ourselves. He will supply for our insufficiencies.

Always in union of prayer and sacrifice near Our Lord.

Sister Lucia dos Santos, I.C.D.

I had gone to Aljustrel, as I said, to visit Maria dos Anjos; and she spoke freely to me of her recollections of her own mother (Maria Rosa) during the time of the apparitions:

"My mother did not want to believe that our Lady was appearing to the three children, at least not to Lucia. She said, 'If it is true that our Lady is appearing, it will spread to the ends of the world.' Mother believed that Lucia was seeing the Lady only after [she herself witnessed] the miracle of the sun.

"On the 13th, people would see a star coming from the east and going over the holm-oak tree. I myself saw the star once and also the falling of the flowers [September 13, 1917]. They were tiny little white flowers, like flowers from the olive trees. People who had umbrellas tried to catch them, but they never did. Everybody wanted to catch them with their hands, but nobody did. They would disappear. They were always in the air. There were many flowers. I saw the raining of the flowers even better than the star. The star would come at midday. It would look like a night star. It was small. It would come and disappear in the direction of the tree.

"Then my doubts whether Lucia was telling the truth began to disappear."

I recorded Maria's statements in English translation and had them translated back into Portuguese for her to check the accuracy. She beamed with delight to recall these events, and did so with great clarity of mind. A crowd gathered around to listen to our conversation. Asking Maria if she would sign the notes I had made of what she had told me, she replied that she could not sign because she never went to school. She signed an "X" for her signature.

Then she added: "Recently a man came to me. I asked, 'Where did you come from?' He said, 'I came from the end of the world.' I said, 'That must be what my mother meant, "The message would go to the end of the world." ' "

When I asked Maria to pray for me and my work with young people (the

Cadets of Our Lady of Fatima), she answered: "We should pray for one another and for peace in the world. Young people especially need prayer. . . . We must pray for peace in the world."

Remembering more things she wished to share with me, Maria added that she did not know for certain on which rock of the well the angel had stood. "I was so anxious to know on which rock, and when Sister Lucia came to Fatima in 1946 and was pointing it out, at that moment someone pushed me and I didn't get to see. It was as if it was supposed to be that way. Later I went to see Sister Lucia and asked her, 'Which rock?' She said, 'You already know too much,' and she wouldn't tell me. Good thing, or I might have told someone and people would haul off the rock."

Each time I returned to Aljustrel, if the weather was good, when the sun had risen high, I'd find Maria dos Anjos seated in front of the family residence—where the Santos family lived in 1917 at the time of the apparitions. Each year, I've wondered whether I would still find her there.

On July 22, 1980, I again interviewed her.

"Maria, how old are you?"

"This August 15, I will be 89 years old."

"How many brothers and sisters in your family?"

"There were seven children. I was the oldest of seven, and Lucia the youngest."

"Are any brothers and sisters living besides you and Sister Lucia?"

"All are dead except Caroline."

"When did you last talk to Sister Lucia?"

"About a year ago. The Holy Father has given the immediate family permission to see Lucia anytime. I cannot walk now. I broke my hip about a year ago, but before that I had broken the other hip." (She was now able to get about with the aid of a walker.)

"What did you think the first time you heard that Lucia saw the 'beautiful lady' in the Cova?"

"We all thought, including myself, that she was lying. My mother didn't believe it until the miracle of the sun. All my family thought it was not true. After the miracle of the sun, my mother came home and said, 'There was the miracle so I could believe'; and after that, Mother never doubted."

"Had you been close to Lucia before the apparitions?"

"I used to be like a mother to Lucia, as I was the oldest. I was married and had two children at the time of the apparitions. One of my daughters is a professor in a lyceum [that is, a teacher in a secondary school]. Two of my children died. We have to be satisfied with what our Lord gives us. I have six living children. A daughter lives down the street here with ten children. A son also has ten children. They are poor, but all work. I have a son a priest, Father Valinho."

In this photograph taken shortly after Lucia became a Carmelite nun, Maria dos Anjos, Lucia's eldest sister, sits beside Lucia's mother.

"Were you one of the sisters who made fun of Lucia at home?"

"We didn't like what she was saying. We never beat her, although people say that we did. Neighbors beat her."

"But I've heard that your mother took a broom after Lucia."

(Laughter.) "Mother once took the broom after Lucia. Mother could not accept that Lucia would lie. She did hit her at least once with the broom."

"Did you have a strict mother?"

"She was very strict."

"Maria, were you strict with your children?"

"I tried to be strict with my own children, but they were impossible. They are all good Catholics."

"When did you first begin to believe Lucia was actually seeing 'the beautiful Lady from heaven'?"

"The first I began to believe was when I saw the little things like the falling of flowers and the star [September 13, 1917]. I did not believe firmly until the miracle of the sun."

"Before October 13, 1917, did Lucia say it was the Blessed Virgin Mary who was appearing to her, to Francisco and Jacinta?"

"At first they said it was a 'beautiful lady from heaven'; but after the second apparition Lucia said it was our Lady."

"Were you present on October 13, 1917, at the miracle of the sun? And can you describe what you saw?"

"Yes, I was there. It rained. There were many people. About noon, the rain stopped. We looked at the sun. The sun had lost its brilliance. All of a sudden, the sun started to spin. It seemed to be coming toward the earth. Everybody started to scream and yell. All thought they were going to die."

"Were you frightened?" (Maria laughed at this question.)

"Everybody was very much afraid. Everyone knelt and asked our Lord's forgiveness, because they all thought they were going to die. I was among them. I thought the same thing."

"Do you remember how the crowd acted when the clocks said twelve noon according to Portuguese 'war time' and the Lady had not yet appeared?"

"No."

(Others have reported that the crowd had begun to murmur and that many thought no miracle was going to happen as they waited in the rain and mud for an additional hour or more, beyond the anticipated time of the miracle.)

"Do you remember what your home was like when you returned in the late afternoon after the miracle of the sun? There were reports that you returned to find your home miraculously clean after the October 13th miracle."

"No. I do not remember."

"How did your family act toward Lucia after the miracle of the sun?"

"After the miracle of the sun, Mother never treated Lucia badly; but then she believed everything Lucia said. All my family believed then, too. And all the people believed."

"How did Lucia act at home after the family believed the Mother of God had appeared to her?"

"Just like she did before. She did not change."

"What did Lucia do at home during the few years after the visions, before she left for Porto?"

"She continued to be as she was before. She took the sheep to the pasture as before. We never saw her sad before or after the apparitions."

"But I thought your parents had to sell the sheep after the apparitions."

"People came and asked Lucia to stay with them for a few days. A priest once took Lucia for two or three days to ask her questions. My parents finally sold the sheep because we had no one to take care of them. The people kept coming [to see Lucia and ask questions], and after that they had to sell the sheep."

"When did your father first believe in the Fatima events?"

"He didn't care. He did not say a word for or against. My father would say when people asked questions: 'I don't know anything about these things. These things are for women.' My father believed after the miracle of the sun. We all believed then. Everyone saw that it was not something of earth but of God."

"Why did your father not go to Mass in the parish church of St. Anthony's in Fatima?" It was a question about a delicate matter, and Maria did not desire to answer, apparently out of respect for the priesthood.

"It was not only my father. We all [went elsewhere] at times. There was a little chapel not far away, and we would go there too because of the difference in times of the Masses."

"Where have you gone to Mass through all these years?"

"St. Anthony's Parish Church. My mother never allowed anyone not to assist at Mass. At present I can only watch holy Mass on television."

"Has the Blessed Virgin Mary ever manifested any special supernatural favors to you since the apparitions?"

"No. We were poor and we stayed poor. We never experienced anything special."

And it is true. The family members continued to live in most humble surroundings, profiting nothing financially from the apparitions and consequent world interest. In more recent years, Maria has lived in a humble house, a little better in condition than the original family house, directly across the narrow street in Aljustrel. Someone has provided her with a television, which is seldom used. On warm summer days, she spends most of the day in a chair outside her house. She merely observes the pilgrims who come to Aljustrel, and is kind to anyone who speaks to her.

ii

It is difficult for Americans and others of affluent societies to appreciate the simplicity and naturalness of the people of the mountain areas of Portugal even to the present day; and even more so, those who have survived from the time of the apparitions. They are totally unaffected by the outside world in their thinking and attitudes.

Father John De Marchi, I.M.C., who served for a time as parish priest at Fatima, wrote the now-famous book *Fatima: The Facts* as the fruit of his having had the opportunity to question, at length and undisturbed, the many reliable witnesses of events associated with the apparitions. He once told me that the parents of Jacinta and Francisco and those of Lucia were the type for whom it would have been psychologically impossible to lie or concoct in their imaginations the events surrounding the apparitions. The same was true of the children and the people of the parish in general. "Perhaps," he noted, "it would be possible for people from America or Italy, but not for these people."

He has written: "Every Sunday afternoon for six consecutive months, after the recitation of the Rosary at the Shrine, Ti Marto (Senhor Pedro Manuel Marto, father of Jacinta and Francisco) came and talked to us of his Jacinta and Francisco; of 'his Reverence [the parish priest] who didn't believe and didn't let us believe either'; of the Mayor of Ourém, etc.; all this with a conscientiousness and scrupulous care for truth remarkable in one already old and worn with work. 'We must not exaggerate or squeeze more out of things than was there,' he frequently remarked. He rarely hears a chapter or passage read from a book on Fatima without correcting some detail or adding some missing fact. 'It wasn't exactly like that!' he would say. And then there followed a torrent of detail and reminiscence which often caused the subject under discussion to be completely forgotten. . . .

"When I asked him if he did not feel a certain pride in being the father of such privileged children, he replied with the utmost simplicity: 'Our Lady chose this part of the world and she might have appeared to others. They just happened to be mine!'"

The same simplicity is evident in all the surviving family members of the three children in Aljustrel, including Maria dos Anjos and John Marto, brother of Jacinta and Francisco. John has lived happily in extreme poverty (measured by affluent European or American standards) and will doubtless so live until death.

I once asked Maria, "How do you feel today about what happened in the life of your sister, Sister Lucia?" "I don't feel any different," she replied matter-of-factly.

The country folk of the Sierra de Aire speak a characteristically blunt, graphic language. They are without affectations, and are refreshingly direct in their speech. This quality does not translate well into English. It is easy to see why the Mother of God should pick such an honest, simple, direct type of people as recipients of her message to the world.

When I asked Maria, "Would you summarize your understanding of the Fatima Message?" she became very serious. "There is much to be done," she said, "and people must heed what our Lady has said. Our Lady had asked for the conversion of sinners, and it hasn't been done. I can't explain what I feel. I say all 15 mysteries of the Rosary each day for the conversion of sinners and for peace in the world. I pray for all the people."

As a parting farewell that day (July 22, 1980), Maria added: "I can neither read nor write, but I am happy."

The responses I have received during my conversations with Maria dos Anjos and others who were close to the 1917 events have all been consistent with what others have reported.

Father De Marchi, who became so well acquainted with the people of the Fatima parish during the 1940s, said of them, "They were the type who could neither read nor write, but could listen to a sermon and relate it back to you verbatim." Having little of the world to distract them, having to rely so much on their memories, they possessed not only a power of recall but a keen acumen, even in advanced age.

iii

The home of Maria dos Anjos stands less than 50 feet from the old family house where her parents, Antonio and Maria Rosa Santos, had raised their seven children. Just down the narrow street is the home in which Pedro Manuel "Ti" Marto and his wife, Olimpia, had reared their children. Their son Jon and his wife still live in the Santos house, "guarding" it.

"Do you remember the time your mother was very sick," I asked Maria dos

Anjos, "and you told Lucia to go to the Cova if our Lady had appeared there, and to ask our Lady to make your mother well because you feared your mother would die?"

"I was already married at that time," Maria began. "My sister Gloria came to tell me that my mother was very ill and 'we think she is going to die.' I came immediately. I found all of my brothers and sisters around my mother's bed, and they were crying.

"I said to Lucia, 'If it is true that our Lady is appearing to you, why don't you ask her to cure our mother? Father is already dead, and if Mother dies, we'll all be orphans.' Lucia said nothing. She left and went to the Cova.

"A little while later, Lucia came home with a handful of earth. She gave it to me and said, 'Put this in a cup. Put some water on it, and give it to Mother to drink.'

"Mother said, 'What kind of water is this? It has a very clay color.' Lucia said to Mother, 'Drink it.' Mother did. A little while later, Mother was well.

"Lucy told us after Mother got well, 'I made a promise to our Lady that if Mother would recover, then for nine days we would go to the Cova, say the Rosary on our knees, going on our knees. ...'" (The practice of saying the Rosary while "walking" on one's knees from the large Cross at one end of the Sanctuary area to the Capelinha is common among pilgrims to Fatima.)

Maria suddenly remembered something about Jacinta she wished to share, and she changed the topic accordingly. "One day I went to the well to get water." (This is the well behind the Santos home, where in 1916 the angel appeared to the three children the second time.) "I left the three children, Lucia, Jacinta, and Francisco, by themselves in the house. When I came back, I found the crucifix in the middle of the room and the three children around it. I scolded them that they should not play with holy things. Jacinta got up, put her arms around me, and said, 'Don't scold the others. I did it.'" Lucia, in her first *Memoir*, had recalled the same incident:

As I said before, one of her favorite games was that of forfeits. As your Excellency undoubtedly knows, the winner commands the loser to do whatever he or she pleases. Jacinta liked to command the loser to run after a butterfly and catch it. Other times, she ordered him or her to look for any flower she chose and bring it to her. One day we were playing this in my parents' house and I won, so I got the right to command her. My brother was sitting at a table writing, and I ordered Jacinta to hug and kiss him, but she retorted, "This, no! Tell me to do something else. Why don't you make me give a kiss to our Lord over there?" There was a crucifix hanging on the wall. "All right," I answered. "Get up on a chair, bring Him here, and on your knees give Him three hugs and three kisses; one for Francisco, one for me, and another for yourself."

"To our Lord I give as many as you like," she said. Running to take down the crucifix, she kissed and embraced Him so fervently, I never forgot.

Then, gazing at the figure of our Lord, she asked, "Why is our Lord nailed to a cross?"

"Because He died for love of us," I said.

"Tell me how it happened," she asked.

At soirée, my mother used to tell tales. Among my father's and older sisters' stories about enchanted fairies, golden princesses, royal little doves, my mother would always seize the opportunity to tell our Lord's Passion or St. John's martyrdom, etc., so I knew the story of our Lord's Passion. As it was enough for me to have heard the stories once to be able to repeat them in detail, I began to tell my companions word for word our Lord's story, as I used to call it.

When my sister [Maria] passed by us and saw the crucifix in our hands, she took it from us and scolded me, forbidding me to handle Holy Images. Jacinta got up and approached my sister, saying, "Maria, don't scold her, it was I. But I will not do it any more." My sister caressed her and told us to go and play outdoors for there was nothing left in its place. So we went to continue our story over by the well I previously spoke about. As it was hidden by some chestnut trees, a clump of stones and brambles, we chose, some years later, for this to be a cell of our colloquies and fervent prayers. And, your Excellency, to tell you all the truth, sometimes with very bitter tears.

"What kind of child was Jacinta?" I asked Maria about her niece, knowing that the sanctity of Jacinta and Francisco was at that time being studied by the Holy See as a step toward their beatification and eventual canonization.

"She was a normal child," came the answer, "like all other children. She was very pretty. To us she was like other children. When they were little, the children used to play together. One day, I found them at the brick wall behind the house." (I glanced at the Santos house, where the two children and Lucia often played together.) "They had one of the boys dressed in black. They were kneeling all around him, saying that he was a priest. He was preaching to them. Lucia, Jacinta, and Francisco were among the other children around the boy dressed in black."

I thought: here on this mountaintop of the Sierra de Aire, the family and the faith are at the very center of life. Even in their games, the children live and breathe their faith.

"Was Jacinta spoiled?" I asked.

"She was the youngest, and everyone paid attention to her. Lucia was not spoiled. She was very quiet, especially when we did not believe what she was telling us of our Lady's appearances. She never said a word, no matter how we scolded her."

I asked, gingerly, whether Maria recalled any time when she had hurt Lucia.

"Yes. We all did. We all scolded Lucia all the time. One night, when we all were telling Lucia, 'It is not true that our Lady is appearing to you, and you are lying'—in the midst of all this, my father entered. He listened to us for a time. Then he said to Lucia, '*Do* you see her?'' If you do see her, say yes. If you don't, don't lie about it.' He turned and left the house. After that, all quieted down."

"Was not your father the one who was most kind to Lucia during the months of the apparitions, when others were not believing and were accusing Lucia?"

"Yes. He was the one who seemed to care for Lucia the best. He never scolded her."

"Through these years that you have gone to visit Lucia—knowing that she has continued to receive some additional messages from our Lady and our Lord—how do you feel about her as your sister?"

"I cannot express myself. We are not proud about it. We do not brag about it." (During a previous interview, Maria had used the same words, "I cannot express myself.")

"Are you happy about it?"

"Our Lady did not come to my family. She came with reference to the whole world."

"Why do you think God and the Blessed Virgin Mary chose one of your family to receive a message for the world?"

"We never think of it in terms that our Lady came to one of our family. She came for the whole world."

"Don't you think your mother should receive much credit for forming her family, including Lucia, so strong in the faith?"

"Yes. I remember my mother telling Lucia, 'No one in my family ever lied. And now you bring shame upon me by lying.' Lucia never said a word [in self-defense]. Mother was very active in religious organizations. One organization that she was active in was the Society of the Sacred Heart. She was president for quite a few years and as long as she was able.

"When my mother became too old to be president, she went to the parish priest and said that she was resigning because of age. The priest said, 'You have daughters who could take over. So I became president, and my name is still on the honorary list as president of the Society of the Sacred Heart."

"Tell me about Francisco."

"I did not know Francisco any better than [I knew] the other children. His father used to say, 'He's a bad boy.' That was because, one time, when one of his older brothers [John] was sleeping in a chair with his mouth open, Francisco tried to drop a chip of wood into his mouth."

When I spoke with Maria in August of 1980, I was privileged to introduce Brother Gino of San Vittorino, a stigmatic, to her. Her eyesight having grown very dim, she paid little attention to him, no doubt thinking he was another of the many hundreds of thousands who come each year to Fatima and pass through the streets of Aljustrel. When I brought his name more clearly to her attention, she recognized it at once and said: "I've heard about you, and I've been wanting to meet you." The two of them looked admiringly at each other, each feeling privileged to have met the other.

On each of my annual visits to Fatima, a highlight has been the chance to visit with sober-faced John Marto and his smiling wife, Amelia. Their small house had once been the home of the affectionate family of John's parents, "Ti" and Olimpia Marto, the parents also of Jacinta and Francisco.

iv

Ti Marto, who had a way with words, gave evidence of abundant common sense and wisdom, even if he saw little use for much formal education. A typical example of his manner was his reply to a questioner who had noticed the children's absence on that August 13th (when the mayor had taken them to Ourém for "questioning"): "I know absolutely nothing. . . . Nobody knows where they are. On the day when they were taken, my stepson, Antonio, and some other lads went there and said they saw them playing on the veranda of the mayor's house. That was the last I heard." Recalling that incident in later years, he said to Father De Marchi:

> *The words were hardly out of my mouth when I heard someone say: "Look, Ti Marto, they're on the veranda of the presbytery!" I hardly knew how I got there, but I rushed up and hugged my Jacinta. I picked her up—I can even remember now that I sat her on my right arm. . . . I just couldn't speak. The tears poured down my face and made Jacinta's all wet. Then Francisco and Lucia ran up to me, crying: "Father, Uncle, give us your blessing!" At that moment there appeared a funny little official, a man who was in service to the mayor, and he shook and trembled in the most extraordinary way. I had never seen anything like it! He said, "Well, here are your children." Then I couldn't help myself and burst out: "This might have had a sorry ending and it's not your fault if it didn't. You wanted them to say they were lying and you couldn't make them. And even if you had made them I should have told the truth!"*
>
> *Then we heard a tremendous noise in the square. The people were waving and shouting, you never heard such a noise. Father Ferreira, who was in the church, went at once to the house, up the steps, and thinking it was I who was causing the riot, said: "Oh, Senhor Manuel, it is you making all this trouble?" But I knew how to answer him, too, and went inside. Then I turned to the people and, with Jacinta still in my arms, shouted: "Be quiet, all of you! Some of you are shouting against the mayor, some against the priest and the regedor, but it all comes from lack of faith and is allowed by God."*

Father Ferreira, who had heard it all, was satisfied, and said from the win-dow: "Senhor Marto is quite right, quite right."

At this moment the mayor arrived and showed himself to the people, saying to me: "That's enough, Senhor Marto." And I answered: "It's all right, it's all right, nothing has happened." Then he went to Father Ferreira's office, called me in, and said to the priest: "I prefer Abobora's [Lucia's father's] con-versation, but I must see Marto, too."

Then Father Ferreira said: "Mr. Mayor, we cannot do without religion!"

As Senhor Santos was leaving, he asked me to go and have a glass of wine with him but I refused. But just then I saw a group of boys below, armed with sticks, and I thought to myself that at this stage it would be better to have no more trouble, so I said to the mayor: "After all, sir, perhaps I'll accept your of-fer."

He thanked me kindly because he was beginning to realize the feeling against him and that things were likely to warm up. At the bottom of the stairs he said:

"You can be sure that I treated the children well."

"That's all right, sir, it's not I but the people who seem to want to know that."

At that moment the children came down the steps and set off for the Cova da Iria, where, they said, they were going to pray. The people began to disperse slowly, and I went with the mayor into the tavern, where he ordered wine and bread and cheese to be brought. He started a silly conversation that didn't in-terest me at all, but at a certain point he tried to make me think that the chil-dren had told him the secret. And I said, without moving a muscle: "All right, all right. As they wouldn't tell it to their father or mother, it's natural that they should tell it to you."

When we came out, the carriage was at the door. I said good-bye; but as I had to go to the post, which was some way along the road to the town, he made me get in and go along with him although it was so near. I got in and some-body shouted: "There goes Ti Marto! He's talked too much and [the mayor is] taking him to prison!"

v

Shortly after the day of the children's release, they were taking the sheep to pasture in the late afternoon. As they passed by the Marto house, Jacinta was called into the house by her mother, who asked her to stay home and help her. So it happened that this time Lucia, Francisco, and his brother John were to-gether. About four o'clock, Lucia began to notice some unusual changes in their surroundings.

I felt something supernatural approaching and enveloping us. Suspecting that our Lady was coming, and feeling sorry that Jacinta should miss seeing her, we asked John to go and call her. As he did not want to go, I offered him two coins and he ran off.

Years later, during one of my visits, I gave John two coins in remembrance of the time Lucia "bought him off" so he would agree to fetch Jacinta—who joined Lucia and Francisco just in time for our Lady's appearance at Valinhos. John humbly accepted the coins for the sake of the memory.

On July 23, 1980, I had a long conversation with John Marto in his home. His directness and simplicity of manner reflect the very qualities described by Father Manuel Numes Formigão, Father John De Marchi, and other authors who have written of the Fatima children.

At that time, John Marto, well into his seventies, still worked in the fields each day; so I had to arrange to meet him when he would be home from work. The day before I spoke with him, I asked his granddaughter when Grandfather John would be home, and she said, "When he is finished."

"John, how many brothers and sisters do you have?"

"Nine counting me. Antonio, Manuel, Joseph, a sister Theresa, who died when she was a few months old; Florinda, Theresa (another sister, named after the one who had died), John, Francisco, and Jacinta."

"Any living members of the family besides you, John?"

"Joseph, who is 81, and myself, 74 years of age."

"How much older were you than Francisco?"

"Two years."

"Did Jacinta and Francisco ever talk about the apparitions?"

"Personally not to me, but when people would come and ask them questions, then I would hear about it."

"Were you not curious to ask them questions about the apparitions yourself?"

"No."

"Did you think they were holier than you because they had the apparitions?"

"It did not impress me. When I would see Francisco saying the Rosary many times, this would make me think he was holier than I."

"How often would you see him saying the Rosary?"

"I would see him saying the Rosary all day long."

"Did you try to imitate him in that?"

"At times I would imitate him in saying the Rosary, but at times I would leave him so that I could not see him praying the Rosary."

"Did your relationship with Francisco change after the apparitions?"

"No. All was the same."

"Did you play games with him after the apparitions?"

"Very little before or after. We played very little in those days. At that time I already worked on a farm."

John Marto—brother of Francisco and Jacinta—at the doorway of the family home.

"When did you first believe that the Blessed Virgin Mary was appearing to Jacinta and Francisco?"

"At first we all thought they were lying, but we believed after the miracle of the sun."

"But I thought your father believed immediately."

"My father never said to anyone he believed the children; but after a year or two he admitted that he had believed them immediately. This was the case when Jacinta came home in May and said she saw a beautiful lady in the Cova."

"Did you believe her at first, John?"

"No."

"How did your parents react to the first reports that the Blessed Virgin Mary was appearing to Jacinta and Francisco?"

"On the 12th of the month, Jacinta and Francisco would ask their mother to go with them to the Cova, and she would say: 'No. She isn't appearing to me, so I'm not going to go.' So she did not go. In the beginning, my father did not go to the Cova because he said that if he went it would be bad and if he did not go it would be bad. So instead, he went to the market so he would not be here [at home]. He did not go to the Cova until August."

"But it was in August that the children were in jail on the 13th?"

"He went to the Cova alone. When it was time for our Lady to come, he saw a cloud. It was very hot. All of a sudden there was a wind, and then they smelled perfume as the wind passed them. My father did not know that the children had been kidnapped and taken to the Ourém jail. Men had come and told my parents that they would take the children [Jacinta, Francisco, and Lucia] to the Cova. So the children went with them; but instead of going to the Cova, they went to the church; and there was a car waiting at the church, and from there they took the children to jail." (This was the reason why people thought the parish pastor, Rev. Manuel Marques Ferreira, was involved in the mayor's kidnapping plot.)

"Did you come back to Valinhos with Jacinta that day in August when Lucia gave you a couple of coins to go call Jacinta because our Lady was coming?"

"Lucia, Francisco, and I went to Valinhos with the sheep. Jacinta stayed home. Lucia noticed that something was going to happen, and so she asked me to go get Jacinta. I left fast for Jacinta and returned with her to Valinhos. I didn't see anything, and I thought they did not see anything either. The children told the family later that the Lady had told them not to be afraid and to continue to go to the Cova on the 13th."

John's recollections of those events of 1917 are remarkably in agreement with the accounts given in Lucia's *Memoirs* and other early, scholarly reports. As we talked, John sat in a chair in the living room of the home, answering my questions with great patience, despite the many interruptions caused by pilgrims coming in to see the bedrooms of Jacinta and Francisco.

"But couldn't you tell the children at Valinhos were in ecstasy? Didn't you notice that they were talking to someone?"

"No."

"Were you very close to Francisco as a brother?"

"No."

"Did your family life change after the apparitions?"

"It continued the same way."

"Were you present October 13, 1917, to see the miracle of the sun?"

"I stayed in the house. After the miracle of the sun, the people came here to the house and said: 'It is true. The Blessed Mother has appeared to the children.' Mother and Father went to the Cova that day."

vi

John's memory is corroborated by his father's testimony (as recorded by Father De Marchi):

A few days before October 13th, Fr. Poctas, parish priest of Mos, and one of his parishioners came to see us to try to make the children deny what they had said.

By the time I arrived back home, they had already questioned Francisco but without any result. They wanted to talk to the other two but they had gone to Boleiros with a donkey to get some lime. Although I told them that they would be back before long, they went to find them with my John. It was not long before they all came back and I met them at the house of Lucia's sister, Maria dos Anjos. Then and there Fr. Poctas attacked Lucia: "Look here, child, you're just going to tell me that all this is stuff and nonsense and if you don't I will say so myself and tell everyone else, too. People believe me and, besides, they are going to the Cova to destroy everything and you won't escape either."

Lucia didn't say a word so I turned to Fr. Poctas and said: "Yes, that's just what we ought to do and then nobody will come here on the 13th. It would be the best thing that could happen."

I was very angry, and Jacinta, who never liked to see anyone angry, suddenly disappeared. I turned to Fr. Poctas and said: "In any case, please leave the children alone. There's nothing to prevent your doing what you like about it."

Then the other man said furiously: "This is nothing less than witchcraft. The same thing happened with a servant of mine some time ago, and when she got the idea into her head, nothing on earth could rid her of it!"

Without more ado we all went back to the house and found Jacinta on the doorstep playing with a child about her own age.

"Listen, Jacinta," said Fr. Poctas again, "Haven't you anything to say? You know Lucia has told us everything, and now we know that it's all a lie."

"Lucia never said that," replied Jacinta firmly.

And though he insisted, she stood firm and repeated that Lucia had said nothing. I could see that they were all surprised at Jacinta's firmness; I even thought they believed in the Apparitions, and at one moment the other man pulled a coin out of his pocket and tried to give it to Jacinta.

"You must not do that!" I told him.

"Surely I can give something to John then!"

"It's not necessary, but if you like you can give it to him."

When they were leaving, Fr. Poctas turned to me and said: "Congratulations, you have played your part well!"

"Well or ill, that's my way," I answered. "You haven't succeeded in making the children deny their story, but even if you had I should still believe in them!"

While Ti Marto was calm and convinced, his wife, Olimpia, was upset because priests and many other people had said things would not go well on October 13th.

John's memory about his father's not saying to anyone that he believed the children until a year or two later is a reflection of his father's caution in dealing with the public. For, as Ti Marto reported to Father De Marchi about the events of October 13: "When they came to leave, I got ready to go with the children; but at that moment a neighbor came up to me and whispered: 'Better not go, Ti Marto. You might be attacked. They won't hurt the children because they're so small, but with you it's another matter!' 'But I am going, because I have faith in it! ... I'm not at all afraid and am quite sure that everything will go off all right.' "

When I asked John, in 1980, to share with me his memories and impressions of Jacinta, he said: "She was very humble and obedient. If her mother would tell her to sit in one spot, she would not move until her mother gave her permission. She liked to play and to dance. She was very happy."

"Was she not spoiled after the apparitions?"

"No, but when children came and wanted to play with her, if anyone said a word she thought was not proper, she would send them home."

"Did she ever correct you?"

"No."

"What would you think if the Church declared Jacinta a saint?"

"I believe she should be a saint."

"Why?"

"I dreamt that Jacinta told me that I should say the Rosary with my brothers and sisters so that they would get along together. This was about 10 years after she died."

"And that convinces you she should be canonized a saint?"

"I think, 'yes.'"

"Did Jacinta ever appear to you?"

"Only in a dream."

"Are you convinced that the dream was of heaven?"

"I believe, 'yes.'"

I asked him again about Francisco—what sort of person he was.

"I think Francisco was a humble boy. When Francisco was ill, he wouldn't tell anyone he was in pain. He would keep it to himself."

"Did you see the light by Francisco's door just before he died?"

"No."

"Do you think Francisco should be declared a saint by the Church?"

"I think, 'yes.'"

"Why?"

"I have faith that Francisco will become a saint."

"Soon?"

"I don't know."

"Do you say the Rosary daily, John?"

"Yes." ...

"John, would you summarize the message of Fatima as you understand it?"

"I understand that the message of Our Lady of Fatima is to say the Rosary daily . . . ," he began. Then suddenly he rose from his chair and went into Francisco's bedroom. He returned with a small card, on which he had printed a message; he had apparently hung the card on a string in Francisco's room. He sat down and handed me the card. "I wrote this."

The card read: *Amigo: Se queres cumprir a primeira mensagem de Fatima, REZA O TERCO TODOS OS DIAS* (Friend: if you want to live the first message of Fatima, say the Rosary daily). John said to me: "It was my idea to write this. I put it there for the pilgrims to see." He added: "The second message as I understand it is the five First Saturdays."

"How has the Fatima message changed your life?"

"I go to Mass . . . confession . . . pray the Rosary daily."

"How many children did you have?"

"Four."

"Did you try to teach them the Fatima message?"

"I taught them to go to Holy Mass, confession, to say the Rosary. They are all good Catholics."

vii

A few days later, July 26, in late morning, I returned to Aljustrel with two fellow Americans, Jack and Betty Barlow. Greeting us, John proudly announced, "I've already been to Ourém and back with my donkey and cart."

"Did you go to get groceries?"

"No." He motioned for us to follow him to a shed across a narrow road from his house. There he proudly showed us a brown goat he had bought that morning in Ourém, some hours' journey away by cart.

"It's too young yet to give milk," John said to us.

After we had admired the goat, John led us back across the street to a farmyard immediately beside the house, where he then proudly showed us his donkey—a rather large and healthy-looking creature as far as donkeys go; and there too we saw the cart in which he had gone to Ourém that morning.

It struck me again that this was the same house and farmyard that Jacinta and Francisco knew, and that John and his wife still lived in the same manner as their parents had—working in the fields, milking goats, traveling by donkey cart. The comings and goings of thousands of pilgrims from throughout the world had not affected these people in the least. As Canon Galamba once said to me, "John now looks like his father, Ti Marto."

John agreed to pose with me beside his donkey for a photograph. But the donkey was not in agreement; he bucked, ran back into a small building, and refused to come to the gate for the picture. So John went across the street and picked up a small pear, and used it to coax the donkey to the gate. His strategy worked, and the picture was taken.

Just then John's wife, Amelia, arrived on the scene. Seeing Jack with his camera, but not knowing the picture had already been taken, she began to scold her husband quite severely for not getting the donkey some fruit so as to bring the beast out on the road to please us so we could have a picture. Amelia had been sick of late, and she was not in her best mood.

John listened in silence to his wife's scolding, but said nothing, declining to explain to her that the picture had already been taken. . . .

When I returned to Aljustrel and Fatima in July-August 1981, John Marto recognized me immediately. I had, as usual, many young people with me, and I persuaded John to coax the donkey to cooperate while photographs were taken. I asked about the goat that John had just bought at the time of my previous visit. He led the goat out into the road; and Amelia said, "It doesn't give milk. All it does is eat and get fat."

"Does she have little ones?" I asked.

"No."

"Maybe she needs to have little ones before she will give milk," I suggested.

No response, but sober looks from John and Amelia.

V. Canon Galamba and Others

Americans differ psychologically," the venerable old priest said to me. "It is difficult for them to 'get' Fatima. They want to get it in five minutes, and some have only an hour or two to spend here. They leave having missed what it is all about."

This learned and humble theologian could not understand why I wanted to interview him, that July 25, 1980.

"I have many questions," I began.

Jokingly he said, "Are you from the CIA?" Yet the good old priest was most gracious in answering my questions, and even offered lunch.

He asked whether American travel agencies might be persuaded to prepare Americans for pilgrimage to Fatima, so that they would come not merely as sightseeing tourists but as pilgrims in fact—for study, prayer, and reflection on the Fatima message. I admitted it was a difficult task. Most travel agencies are not in the business to promote religion, but to make money. They sell noise. They are not interested in pilgrims' having time to reflect, but in keeping them occupied every minute. Things must move fast. On the buses that bring American travelers to Fatima, the Portuguese guides talk mostly of secular matters; that is what they are paid for. I had learned from experience that there is little silence as one passes through the peaceful countryside.

Dr. Conego José—commonly known as Canon Galamba—listened patiently to my complaint. He had been closely involved with the phenomenon of Fatima for nearly 50 years, as investigator, promoter, and historian.

i

The *Memōrias e Cartas da Irmā Lūcia,* published in Porto in 1973, tells us that on September 12, 1935, when the corpse of Jacinta was removed from Vila Nova de Ourém to Fatima, "the casket was opened and the face of Jacinta looked somewhat preserved. A photograph was taken, and the Bishop of Leiria, José Alves Correia da Silva, sent a copy to Lucia, who thanked him with a letter in which she made mention of her cousin's virtues. This fact, as I mentioned in an earlier chapter, moved the bishop to order her to write everything she could remember about Jacinta's life. What the official notes in the memoirs do not say is that it was Canon Galamba who persuaded the bishop to have her write. Lucia's four *Memoirs* were the eventual result.

77

Canon Galamba has a rich personality and has done extraordinary work during his more than 50 years as a priest. Born in Aldeia Nova, the parish of Olival, Council of Vila Nova de Ourém, he entered the Patriarchate Seminary of Santarém in 1914, where he completed his preparatory studies. He attended the Gregorian University of Rome, whence he returned in 1924 as doctor of philosophy and bachelor of theology and Canon Law. Ordained on July 11, 1926, in the Cathedral of Leiria, he was assigned to the diocesan seminary as prefect and professor.

In 1933, he organized the weekly newspaper *A Voz do Domingo* (The Voice of Sunday), of which he remained director until 1975. Through the columns he wrote for this paper, he became known as a fighter and teacher in total fidelity to the Church, without betraying discouragement or defeat, regardless of what battles and misunderstandings he had to face.

Besides many other works, Canon Galamba was the diocesan and local assistant of Catholic Action. He founded various homes for women, girls, and boys. He was the impetus for the creation of social works for workmen in rural parishes, and promoted domestic-formation courses. His School of Rural Social Formation, in 20 years' time, prepared more than 300 agents to work in the whole country and foreign lands.

In addition, he gave many spiritual retreats and courses for priests and for laity of all professions and social standings. For six years he was president of the Guild of the Press in Portugal.

He was the second director of the Pious Union of Crusaders of Fatima, and vice-president of the executive commission for the fiftieth anniversary of the apparitions of Fatima in 1967, when Pope Paul VI came to Fatima. For many years he served as president of the Blue Army of Our Lady of Fatima in Portugal. He wrote four books about Jacinta, based on his investigations. Indeed, perhaps no other priest in Portugal has done more to make known the Fatima message than Canon Galamba.

On July 31, 1978, I had previously interviewed him; he was at that time the *diocesan* president-judge for the tribunal for the beatification and canonization of Jacinta. (A year later, the diocesan investigation was completed, and the tribunal of the Holy See began its further investigation of Jacinta's sanctity.)

Canon Galamba emphasized that while the process of investigation for each child was separate, the commission was examining the lives of both Francisco and Jacinta.

I asked him about the fact that Jacinta's body was incorrupt: was that not evidence of her sanctity? He replied: "You know, not every incorruption of a body is a sign of sanctity. We have some incorrupt bodies that belong to common people. But as we knew the life of Jacinta, it was our impression that the cause of incorruption added some sign of the supernatural. We must not give great importance to this fact, because Francisco, her brother, was perhaps a boy of as high virtues in the spirit of prayer and reparation as was Jacinta; but the body of Francisco was absolutely corrupt." Comparing the two examinations of Jacinta's body—both of which he had witnessed—he said: "The face was incorrupt, as the first time. One could not see the fingers the first time. The second time we could recognize that one finger was corrupt.

"You examined the body down to the waist?"

"No, it was just to recognize that it was the body of Jacinta. That's the regular action we must take in the process in the cause of identification. So after seeing that it was the body of Jacinta, we closed everything and we brought it to the Basilica where it is now."

"How much of the body did you look at? Just the head and hands?"

"Yes. The other parts of the body were with clothes."

"Will you open her coffin again?"

"If the Congregation [for the Causes of Saints] agrees, it will write to the bishop to make the [request for exhumation]. At that time, we must 'recognize' a second time, officially, the body of Jacinta, and that of Francisco. We have the bones of Francisco in a special little box."

"In 1938," I said, "Hitler was ready to conquer Spain and Portugal. At the same time the bishops of Portugal were meeting here at Fatima. Do you recall what the bishops' reactions were upon reading the first typewritten manuscript you wrote about Jacinta?"

"I think so. I think that the knowledge of special things about the apparitions and about the lives of Jacinta and Francisco, was the reason why the bishops sought the intercession of the Immaculate Heart of Mary and made the consecration of Portugal [to her] in order to avoid the war and the dangers of our country here."

"Do you think that the cardinals and bishops of Portugal would have made the consecration of Portugal to the Immaculate Heart of Mary if your manuscript had not been read at their meeting and they had not known the details of the apparitions?"

"I think you are right. Really, if they were without this knowledge, they perhaps would not have made the consecration; my bishop knew about some of the petitions of Sister Lucia to the Holy Father for the consecration of the world to the Immaculate Heart of Mary, but not all the bishops did. My bishop knew only because of the letters and the talks between him and Sister Lucia. And perhaps the consecration would not have been made under these conditions if the other bishops had not had access to the manuscript about Jacinta."

The Canon continued: "I think that Sister Lucia is not dreaming. She is very strict in things she writes. Always she wrote only to obey. She told the bishop that it is very difficult for her and that she would like not to write about the apparitions."

"Yet it was you, Canon Galamba, who 'pressured' the bishop to command

Sister Lucia always to write more and more. Why do you think Sister Lucia was so reluctant to write?"

"Well, in the mind of Sister Lucia was always the secret that the children had received from our Lady. It was just between them, our Lady and the children; and you know, a part of the secret was supernatural, and the secrecy was asked by our Lady. Some other parts were secret because of the conversations between the three children. Perhaps, they thought, it is better not to tell anyone about the apparitions. It was Jacinta who gave the knowledge of the apparitions out, but in the mind of Lucia it was always these loving ways of keeping the secret about everything."

"But as you indicated," I countered, "heaven first used Jacinta as the instrument, because she could not keep silent about it. That is how it got out to the world. And then Jacinta said to Lucia before she died, 'When the time comes to make known about the devotion of the Immaculate Heart of Mary, tell all the world.' So it would seem that years after Jacinta was dead, heaven was still using Jacinta as an instrument to get the message of these first two parts of the secret to the world; because if her body had not been exhumed and the face found incorrupt and the picture sent to Lucia, there would not have been the demand that Lucia write *everything*. So Jacinta was still doing her work as an instrument of heaven long after she was dead."

"I understand and I agree with you that it was very small things in the hands of God. It was just the way of heaven, making known all these revelations to the world."

"This really means, then, that if Jacinta's body had not been moved from Ourém and first placed in the vault there, the bishops would not have had the manuscript to read in 1938."

"Perhaps, because Sister Lucia never in this life would have written anything about the apparitions or about Jacinta—all coming from this picture and from the body of Jacinta."

I mentioned that before Sister Lucia wrote anything about the apparitions of the Angel of Peace, the bishop had already given his approval to the apparitions of Mary at Fatima. "Can we accept the three apparitions of the angel as authentic, since there has never been any official Church approval of them?"

Canon Galamba replied that he saw no objection to accepting the angelic apparitions. "General approval about these apparitions now has the status of the formal approbation of the Church. All the people [involved in the investigation of Fatima] now agree with the reality of the apparitions of the angel. We do not have an official approbation, as was made for the apparitions of our Lady. In these documents [giving his approval to the apparitions of Mary], the bishop tells us the apparitions of our Lady were real apparitions, and no word is made about the angel. Today there is implied approbation on the part of all the bishops of Portugal, because each of them agrees to the reality of the apparitions of the angel."

The site of the well behind the Santos house in Aljustrel, where the three children experienced the second apparition of the Angel of Peace in 1916.

"So then we may accept it as certain?"

"I think so. It means that if today we were to make an official process about the apparitions of the angel, we would have only the confirmation of the Conference of the Bishops of Portugal about the reality of the apparitions of the angel. I will make a distinction," he added, "between the devotion and the theological doctrine. We don't need the apparitions of the Angel of Peace at Fatima in order to agree in the Church about the existence of the angels."

The writings of Canon Galamba have been translated into the major languages of the world; his book *Jacinta*, into seven languages. He came to know the families of the three children intimately. He served as the censor for the American movie *The Miracle of Fatima*, which has been seen by audiences throughout the world. In 1946, he escorted the *first* "Pilgrim Virgin Statue" to North America. When that statue was shown to Sister Lucia, she remarked that it most closely resembled our Lady, but that, because the Lady appeared to be "all light," no artist could capture what the children saw.

The gracious old priest, who has worked with youth groups in Portugal for many years, mentioned my book *Catholic Truth for Youth* and asked about my apostolate as national spiritual director for the Blue Army Cadets of Our Lady of Fatima in the United States.

"I think," he said, "that everything we can do for young people is very important in the times in which we are living. Everywhere in the world, young people are going a little away from God in the practice of religion. We must approach them, because the future of religion and the Church is in their hands. After some years, they will be the fathers and mothers of the new generation. If we don't approach them now, what will be the future of religion?"

He gave me excessively high praise for my own work, and when I thanked him, he said, "You have nothing to thank me for. You have to thank God for giving you just this mind and health, and we are asking God to give you the graces you need and also the health because you must have both, supernatural grace and natural health, to go ahead."

ii

I had some difficulty finding an opportunity to meet Msgr. Manuel Alves Guerreiro, confessor at the Basilica in the Cova da Iria. On July 30, 1980, as he was slowly making his way toward home after having spent hours in the Basilica confessional, I literally accosted him. "Monsignor, could I have an interview with you regarding what you witnessed of the Fatima events in 1917?"

In an abrupt tone, he replied, "What for? The accounts written on Fatima are quite complete? You can read all about them in the books."

"That's true, but it won't be many more years before people who witnessed firsthand what happened here, won't be around any longer to interview."

The aged priest, who walked with some difficulty, answered, "That's right." And he sat down on a nearby bench and became most friendly.

"Were you present at the September 13, 1917, apparitions in the Cova?"

"Yes."

"Did you see anything unusual?"

"I saw a star coming from the sun, and it came toward the holm-oak [on which the children said the beautiful Lady from heaven was appearing], and then it disappeared."

"Did it not come from the east?"

"No. It came from the sun. I was in the seminary at the time. A group of seminarians came to the Cova, and they were going to show the people that the events of Fatima were a hoax. The seminarians were joking. The leader of the seminarians was a man who is still alive. In the midst of all this joking, all of a sudden Lucia said, 'Close your umbrellas. She is coming.' It was then that the seminarians saw that it was no hoax. They all knelt and, with tears in their eyes, asked pardon from our Lady."

"What happened that they knew it was no hoax?"

"When Lucia said, 'Close your umbrellas,' a spiritual force passed through us and we fell to our knees. Then, each one of us saw some kind of vision. I saw the star. Each one of the group saw a different vision."

I asked, "Did you see the 'falling of the flowers' that day?"

"No."

"How big was the star?"

"Small." He formed a circle about three inches in diameter with his hands. "It was white as snow."

"Did it move fast?"

"It moved slowly. Before it got to the holm-oak, it disappeared. It came close to the tree and then disappeared."

"Were you in the seminary at Santarém?"

"Yes. The group of seminarians came from Santerém and also from Vila Nova de Ourém, and we came to the Cova together to prove to the people that Fatima was a hoax. But then, every one of the seminarians believed after this without question. We believed immediately."

iii

Among the seminarians who came to the Cova that September 13 was none other than Canon Galamba, who at the time was fourteen years old. With him were colleagues from the parish of Olival. He gave me this description of the scene in the Cova on that occasion:

"The land was covered with bushes, with a few larger trees here and there, and was divided by stone walls, according to the custom of the country, either to mark boundaries or just to clean the soil. We climbed on to a wider one, so as to see better. It was on the slope between the place of the apparitions and the place where today there is a church.

"Lower down, the people gathered around the grotto and the little shepherds, who could hardly be seen.

"I did not notice anything near the place, but after the apparition—I can't say the exact moment—I looked up to the sky, perhaps because someone told me to, and I saw, about a meter above the earth, a sort of luminous globe, which soon began to descend toward the west and, from the horizon, went up again toward the sun.

"We were all very moved. We prayed earnestly, for we-knew-not-what. Everyone present could see the same globe except for a colleague of mine, also a priest now, from Torres Novas. I took him by the arm to show it to him, but at that moment I lost the globe from sight before he could see it; which made him say in tears, 'Why is it that I can't see it?'

"Before or after, but certainly on the same day, we—but I don't know if it was true of all those present—began to see a fall of rose petals or snow drops that came from above and disappeared a little way above our heads, so that we couldn't touch them.

"I didn't see anything else, but it was enough to comfort us; and we left with the certainty, like an intuition, that *there* was the finger of God."

Knowing that seminary authorities are usually very cautious in dealing with private revelations regarding their students and dedicate themselves to forming future priests in the Scriptures, the dogmas of the Church, and the Church Fathers, I asked Monsignor Guerreiro about the reactions of his seminary teachers.

"Dr. Formigão, who is the 'Soul of Fatima,' was our professor," he replied. "Dr. Formigão served to give convictions to the seminarians regarding the events of October 13, 1917. Dr. Formigão himself attended on October 13. Generally we would sing hymns to the Blessed Virgin Mary after that. We seminarians wanted to go to the Cova on October 13, 1917, but the seminary authorities would not permit us."

iv

I have read most of the books about Fatima, but my interviewing of persons who lived near the Cova in 1917 and who knew the families and witnessed some of the events has helped me to understand Fatima as a reality, not as a story told in books.

In Father Antonio Dos Reis, born in 1904, I found a former playmate of Francisco. When I interviewed him on July 28, 1980, he was (like Monsignor Guerreiro) a confessor in the Basilica. He had been a playmate of Francisco's during the year and a half they attended catechism class together. "He was just a natural, normal little boy, no different from other boys."

"What kind of games did you play with Francisco?"

"We played 'Spin-the-Top and Buttons.' We had a square with four smaller squares in it. On each of the squares there was a letter: D, P, T, or R. We would spin the top; and wherever the top would land in one of the squares, we would have to do whatever the letter stood for. D stood for 'do not take the buttons.' P meant to pay (or give up the buttons). T stood for 'take one button.' R meant 'take all.' When our mothers, including Francisco's mother, found their buttons missing, they would pull our ears. Francisco was a lively boy when he played with us. It was after the apparitions that he changed."

"How did he change?"

"He became more pious, more fervent, always ready to pray, more contemplative. He would go to church instead of playing."

"Would you see him with the rosary?"

"I don't remember. Francisco would go to church while the other boys kept playing."

Father Dos Reis had entered the seminary in the year the apparitions occurred. "The exams to get into the seminary were on August 12 and 13, 1917, in Vila Nova de Ourém, where the children were kept in prison in August. I went to visit them on the veranda of the administrator's house. The wife of the administrator was a very good woman, a practicing Catholic. She arranged that some of us children could play with the three children, Jacinta, Francisco, and Lucia. All the other children that came to play are now dead. There were three others besides me."

"Did the three children, when you were playing with them, mention anything about threats from the administrator?"

"No. This was the morning of August 13, 1917. We played with them before the [administrator made any] threats of [putting them in] boiling oil. But we could not be with them for a longer period of time because we had to go for the exams. I was then thirteen years old."

"What did you play with the three children at that time?"

"We were on the first floor of the administrator's house, inside the banister. We just visited."

"Do you remember what you talked about to the three children?"

"Questions children would ask: 'Are you afraid? Did they hit you?' "

"Which one did most of the talking?"

"Lucia. I played twenty minutes or less. At that time, the three children did not know they were prisoners. They did not know what the administrator was going to do to them."

"Why did you ask such questions if they did not know they were prisoners?"

"They knew they had been kidnapped. They did not know yet whether they would be able to go home or what the administrator would do with them."

"Did you ever fight with Francisco?"

"In school, yes, at recreation. Our teacher did not have the Catholic faith. Therefore, the children made fun of Francisco because of the apparitions. Consequently the children would fight with Francisco. They pushed him—things children would do."

"Did he fight back?"

"Francisco was very patient. He did not fight back. He would say nothing. He was silent, like Christ. It was more fighting with words than physical. I pushed him, too. Children take such authority upon themselves. . . . He was a tranquil boy. He wasn't aggressive. I was his friend. We lived two kilometers apart. My village was Boleiros."

"You did not believe Francisco was having apparitions?"

"We did not know. Even the bishop did not believe it at that time."

"Did you hear later of the prodigies that took place in the Cova on August 13th?"

"Later in life, I read of it in books."

"When did you first begin to believe in the apparitions at Fatima?"

"Dr. Manuel Formigão, who was present October 13th, told us the same as one reads in the books about the miracle of the sun."

"What was the attitude of your other professors in the seminary toward Fatima after October 13th?"

"In front of the pupils, they said nothing. I don't know about among themselves."

"How did Jacinta impress you?"

"Jacinta was lively, and she was more pious than Francisco. Definitely. I personally never spoke to Jacinta before or after the apparitions."

"Why do you say Jacinta was more pious?"

"Because of her attitude, the way I saw her, her exterior attitude."

"Describe her 'exterior attitude' as you saw it."

"I saw her only in a group. I had no individual contact with her. I was thirteen, and she was seven."

"But you must have noticed something special to speak now of her exterior attitude?"

"This was [something I noticed] mostly in the catechism classes after the apparitions. After the apparitions, she was more to herself, more contemplative. Whatever our Lady told her, I could see from her way of acting that there was something transpiring within her."

Remembering that Sister Lucia's *Memoirs* state that adults experienced a 'supernatural atmosphere' surrounding the children and that other children too were drawn to their presence, I asked Father Dos Reis: "Did you feel something supernatural when you were in the presence of Jacinta or Francisco?"

"The apparitions had an effect on both of them, and this is what I was able to detect."

"How would one live the Fatima message?"

"By doing what the Blessed Mother has asked. Say the Rosary daily. Make the five Saturdays. Do not sin. Do not offend God, who is already so much offended. Pray for peace. Pray for the Holy Father, and pray to the Immaculate Heart of Mary."

"Do you hear confessions every day here at the Cova?"

"Yes."

"Do you think many sinners are converted here?"

"Yes, but whether they keep to their faith when they go to their homes, I don't know. It's a great mystery."

"When you say 'many' are converted, are you speaking mostly of the Portuguese?"

"Yes, more Portuguese—because Portuguese come here all year long, and pilgrims come from other countries May through October. People who come from foreign countries have usually been to confession before they come here. Sometimes a foreigner is converted here. There are strangers who come here purposely, just for confession. Most foreigners come from Spain and from France.

v

One of the more unusual, and to some extent controversial, conversations I've had with the "Fatima survivors" was that with Laurinda da Silva Santos, who for many years was employed by the Fatima Sanctuary. She spoke mainly of the memories of the exhumations of Jacinta's body. Her testimony should be weighed against the fact that the father of Jacinta, who saw her exhumed body, said that Jacinta appeared "as one grown old," and against the following account by Dr. Lisboa as recorded in Father De Marchi's book *Fatima: The Facts:*

> As soon as [Jacinta's] death became known, various people sent money for the expenses of the funeral, which was fixed for the following day, Sunday, at noon, the body to be taken to one of the cemeteries of Lisbon.
>
> When the coffin left the hospital mortuary, it occurred to me that it might be wiser to have the body deposited in some special place, in case the Apparitions should later be confirmed by the Ecclesiastical Authorities or the general incredulity of the subject be overcome. I, therefore, proposed to have the coffin containing Jacinta's body deposited in the Church of the Holy Angels until its removal to some vault could be arranged.
>
> I then went to see my good friend Dr. Reis, the parish priest, who, however, demurred at the idea of the body remaining in his church, owing to certain difficulties. However, with the help of the Confraternity of the Blessed Sacrament, some of whose members happened to be in the sacristy at the time, Dr. Reis was persuaded to give his permission to let the body remain there. Soon afterward, it arrived and was placed humbly on two stools in the corner of the sacristy.
>
> The news spread quickly, and soon a sort of pilgrimage of believers in Fatima began, the faithful bringing their rosaries and statues to touch Jacinta's dress and to pray by her side. All this profoundly disturbed Dr. Reis, who was averse to his church being used for what might well be a false devotion, and he protested energetically by both word and action, thereby surprising those who knew him as a most kind and courteous priest.
>
> It had finally been decided that the body should be taken to a vault in Vila Nova de Ourém, and matters were accordingly arranged—though this involved a delay of two days, the funeral being fixed for Tuesday at 4 o'clock from the Holy Angels Church to the Rossio Station, and from there by train to Vila Nova de Ourém.
>
> Meanwhile her body remained in the open coffin, which again caused serious anxiety to Dr. Reis, who feared an intervention on the part of the sanitary authorities [in Portugal, not more than 24 hours may elapse between death and burial], and he continued to be worried by the stream of visitors, which he only avoided by locking the coffin in an office.
>
> At last, Dr. Reis, in order to avoid the responsibility of the open coffin and the pilgrims, deposited the body in the confraternity room above the sacristy and handed the key to the firm of undertakers, Antonio Almeida and Co., who had been engaged for the funeral. Senhor Almeida remembers to this day, and in great detail, what passed on that occasion.
>
> In order to satisfy the innumerable requests to visit the body, he remained during the whole of February 23 in the church, accompanying each group of

pilgrims—whose numbers were strictly limited—to the room above, in order to avoid any unseemliness which might occur.

He was deeply impressed by the respect and devotion with which the people approached and kissed the little corpse on the face and the hands, and he remembers very clearly the live pinkness of the cheeks and the beautiful aroma which the body exhaled. Owing to the purulent nature of the disease and the length of time that the body remained unburied, this fact is remarkable.

At last, on February 24, at 11 in the morning, the body was placed in a leaden coffin, which was then sealed. Present at this act were Senhor Almeida, the authorities, and several ladies, among them Senhora Maria Pena. . . .

In the afternoon, which was wet, the funeral took place on foot, in the company of a large crowd. The coffin was finally laid in the vault of Baron Alvaiázere in Vila Nova de Ourém.

I remember that on that day the General Annual Conference of St. Vincent de Paul took place and that I excused my late arrival on account of the work of mercy which had claimed my attention, namely, the burial of one of the seers of Fatima. These words provoked an outburst of mirth on the part of the assembly, composed, as may be imagined, of some of the most prominent Catholics of the capital, among them the Cardinal Patriarch himself, who joined in the laugh at my expense. Later he became a great admirer of Fatima and declared that his desire was to celebrate Mass in the Cova da Iria before he died.

It is interesting to record these curious facts, showing as they do the great reluctance on the part of the great majority of clergy and certain of the laity in Portugal to believe in the events of Fatima. . . .

After all these years, it is a great consolation to me to have been instrumental in arranging that Jacinta, in her last illness, should have been under the care of the best doctors and nurses in a Lisbon hospital where the odious calumny, which has been spread abroad, namely, that the Catholics brought about the deaths of the two younger children in order that they should not be able to contradict Lucia's affirmations [that the Lady in the Cova had said that Jacinta and Francisco would be taken to heaven soon] can be most emphatically repudiated.

Having Dr. Lisbon's account in mind, I asked Laurinda da Silva Santos first about Francisco.

"Did you see Francisco's remains when they were dug up?"

"Yes, I touched his bones. They had dug up another body first but said it was not that of Francisco. They found his body down deeper later [11 months later, in 1952].

"Were his bones still together?"

"No. I watched when they were digging his bones out. The ground was clay. All his bones were full of clay. They placed his bones on the lid of the coffin. I helped clean the clay off Francisco's bones."

"Would you please relate how you came to see the exhumed body of Jacinta?"

"Jacinta's body was in Ourém for 15 years. At the request of Dona Maria Celeste de Cāmare de Vosconcelos, Jacinta's body was transported to Ourém from Lisbon after her death. Dona Maria Celeste asked this because her husband gambled their wealth and lost everything. For this reason, she asked that Jacinta's body be brought into the family vault. While Jacinta's body was in the vault for 15 years, her husband stopped gambling and they regained their wealth. Dona Maria Celeste attributed this to Jacinta's intercession.

"After 15 years, the body of Jacinta was next transported to the Fatima cemetery. It was in the Fatima cemetery until April 30th, 1951 [16 years]. When they exhumed her body on April 30, 1951, they found that the coffin was all rotted, so the bishop [Don José Correia de Silva] had a new coffin brought in from Leiria. In the meantime, Jacinta's body was placed in the Salāo [large public building normally used as a recreation building], and people were allowed to go see it. They would come in one door and go out the other. One lady from Moita Rotunda came and, though we were not allowed to touch the body, she threw her arms over Jacinta's body in the old coffin.

"They had intended to cover Jacinta's body with wax but did not do this because she still had so much flesh. I was working in the Sanctuary, and saw all this. I worked in the Sanctuary for eleven years."

I asked her to continue her account of Jacinta's exhumation.

"The [new] coffin with Jacinta's body was brought to Fatima from the Salāo on the shoulders of six priests. When it arrived at the Basilica, it was already sealed. I had seen the body in the Salāo. I saw the whole body."

"What did the body look like?"

"Her body was small when they exhumed it, and with [exposure to] the air it grew bigger. Jacinta appeared taller than myself, as tall as you." (Laurinda is hardly 4'10"; I am 5'10".) "This is how they found that Jacinta's body grew. When they exhumed her, they had a new coffin made. When the coffin arrived, it was too small, so they had to go back and get a bigger coffin for her. It was an adult-size coffin. Jacinta's body filled this bigger coffin."

"Did Jacinta look like an adult then?"

"Yes."

"Was she beautiful?"

"No, because when they exhumed her, little water pellets had formed under the skin."

"What makes you so certain it was Jacinta's body?"

"Because her mother and father recognized her."

"You saw the body when it was first small?"

"No."

"You only saw the body when it was enlarged?"

"Yes."

"Did they change her clothes?"

"They left them as they were."

"How could she have the same clothes if her body grew from the size of a child to that of an adult?"

"The clothes grew with the body."

"What kind of clothes did she have on?"

"I think they were white."

"How long was her hair?"

"She had a veil on so I did not see her hair clearly."

"Was she holding a rosary?"

"She was still holding the rosary she was buried with, which had been given to her by her parents."

"What color was the rosary?"

"I think brownish."

"How much time was there between the opening of the coffin when her body was still small and your seeing it enlarged?"

"I saw it the following day."

"Are you certain you were not seeing someone else's body?"

"Her parents recognized it."

"What did her parents say when they saw her body enlarged?"

"They were very humble. I did not hear them say anything, but they were very happy to see her. They were happy she was in heaven. They never said she was a saint, but they said anyone who is good goes to heaven."

"The photograph taken of Jacinta's body in the coffin after exhumation—is that before or after the enlargement of her body?"

"I don't know."

"What color was her skin?"

"Brownish. It looked like water blisters under the skin. The doctors wanted to clean her hands, but because of the blisters they did not."

"Did Jacinta's body have more flesh than you and I have?" (Jacinta was hardly more than skin and bones at the time of her death because of her prolonged illness and its nature.)

"She had about as much as I, but not as much as you."

"Was she heavy or lean?"

"I don't know, but it took six priests to carry her to the Basilica in the coffin."

"Is it true that your sister Adalina, who lives outside Porto, was recently cured by the intercession of Jacinta?"

"In the Chapel of Domus Pacis I asked the Blessed Mother to cure my sister Adalina; she had trembling of the limbs, and she was paralyzed on her right side. Two doctors were called. One said: 'She will never recover.' The other brought a brace. When he put the brace on her foot, he said, 'It might make a difference.' In this chapel I promised our Lady that if Adalina could walk to the street without the brace, I would have a novena of Masses offered for the conversion of sinners and for the intention of Jacinta's canonization. I telephoned my niece the following day, and she told me that my sister had walked to the street.

"My first prayer had only been that my sister could walk. Her right side was paralyzed. Then I made another promise to our Lady, just before Christmas of 1979. I asked our Lady that if through the intercession of Jacinta my sister Adalina would be able to prepare her own food by the first of the year, I would donate 300 escudos for the cause of the beatification of Jacinta and would publish the miracle. When I went to visit Adalina the first of the year, Adalina told me, 'The doctor that was treating me is very much surprised, but since he is not Catholic he did not want to admit it was a miracle. The doctor said, 'It is something I cannot explain.'

"Adalina explained to me what happened. 'I didn't feel well. Then all of a sudden I was able to move my hand and I could use my limbs. The trembling stopped. Everything was normal.'

"I know how she got well. Adalina doesn't know how or why. I went to the Postulator. The secretary of Father Kondor took everything down. I'm disappointed they did not offer all nine Masses [of the novena] right here at the Capelinha as I promised but offered some in the Basilica and in the Consolata Seminary."

I told her, "Don't worry, you kept your part of the agreement."

vi

At Fatima, one meets the great and the humble. But my impression of those who have been *truly* great in the unfolding of events is that they are also humble. In the summer of 1979, when three priests had just finished concelebrating Mass in the Capelinha, I saw a Frenchman who, in great emotion, overcome with tears, attempted to talk to each of the priests who had just concelebrated. He approached me also, with pleading eyes and voice. Neither I nor the other priests could give him the consolation he sought as he stood beside the pillar marking the spot where our Lady of Fatima had appeared, begging to talk to a priest. We did not understand French. A lady who had observed all this, approached and told me what the man was trying to communicate to us priests. "Father, this man was just converted. Until this moment, he has been a nonbeliever. He has not believed in God. Here at the Capelinha, just now, he was suddenly overcome with the gift of faith. He believes." His happiness at the gift of faith caused the man to break into tears of sorrow, and he wanted the sacraments.

On another occasion—in July 1980—I noticed an unusually large number of Portuguese men making their way, on their knees, along the penitential path and then around the Capelinha. It is common to see *women* making the journey on their knees; this form of doing penance seemed to be "catching on" among the men. That summer, half the pilgrims were male. The men were devout, but they did not sing as loudly as the women, who sing as if their devotion were measured by their volume. One sees many young Portuguese parents going on their knees in penance, with babes in arms. . . .

On a pleasant summer day, while I was praying at the Capelinha, an American woman approached me to have a religious article blessed. I discovered that she did not know we were standing about fifty feet from the site of the apparitions. As I discussed my own longstanding interest in Fatima with her, she became intensely interested in its significance. Our conversation was interrupted when three other members of her party came and told her that the 45 minutes allowed by the itinerary were up. The woman's husband became upset when she told him she would like to return to Fatima and spend some days there in study and prayer. Before I knew what had happened, he pressed something into my hand, saying, "Say Masses for us," and quickly ushered his wife away. In my hand I found two dollars. They do seem to need prayers, I thought. . . .

One evening, near midnight, I was kneeling in the Capelinha. The night coldness was falling upon the Cova da Iria. Yet I felt a special warmth in the open-air Capelinha; for even though the air be bitter cold, I've often found myself asking, in the Cova, "Where did the coldness of the night disappear?"

One such night, the temperature having abruptly fallen with the setting of the sun, I noticed that a bearded young man from France had knelt beside me in the Capelinha. I was moved by his devotion and apparent love for the Mother of God. Somewhat later, when it came time to return to my warm quarters lest I be locked out of Domus Pacis for the night, I decided I could not leave without walking up to the young man and tracing the Sign of the Cross on his forehead and whispering to him that God and His Mother surely love him. He told me he had no money and needed a place to stay the night—and, as it happened, I was the answer to his prayers. "Dear Mother," I said to myself, "you tricked me." Oh well, I felt good about it; and early the next morning I found the same young man praying at the Capelinha. For some reason I thought: could this young man be a future priest who will help bring France back to the faith? . . .

VI. 🌳 The 'Fourth Seer' of Fatima

One sees, crisscrossing the Cova da Iria, religious sisters in blue habits—who have come to be known as "the Blue Sisters." One may see them falling to their knees before the "little chapel," then rising and going to the beautiful chapel built into the center portion of the hospital that sits close behind (that is, just to the west of) the Chapel of Apparitions.

Upon entering the hospital chapel, one is struck with its magnificence despite its small size. On its proportionately high ceiling, the "Madonna as Queen of the Universe" is painted in vivid colors; Mary stands on the earth, with colorful clouds floating in the background, and peoples representing the nations face with her toward the Real Presence of the King of Nations, sacramentally present. On the altar, the Blessed Sacrament is exposed in a monstance; and there, night and day, one will see a "Blue Sister"—now turned white, for she has covered her blue habit with a white veil—upon her knees in Eucharistic adoration and reparation, straight and still. To the rear of the chapel, one sees depicted, in stained glass, the "miracle of the sun."

The "Blue Sisters" are actually the Reparation Sisters of Our Lady of Sorrows of Fatima—whose founder was a priest-theologian, also known in Portugal as "the Man of God and Apostle of Fatima," or even "the Soul of Fatima." I prefer to reserve that last title for our Lady; but it is true that the priest—Dr. (Father) Manuel Nunes Formigão—lived a life so imbued with Mary that one could say Mary was his life.

Father Formigão, canon theologian to the Cardinal Patriarch of Lisbon, not only founded the "Blue Sisters" through an inspiration from our Lady (delivered through the instrumentality of Jacinta) but is also the one who gave the world the first book on the subject of Fatima, in 1921: *Os Episodios Maravilhosos de Fatima* (The Marvelous Events of Fatima). He wrote it under the pen name of Visconde de Montelo. *Episodios* was an account of his official interrogations of Jacinta, Francisco, and Lucia.

i

Sister Mary of the Incarnation, vicar general of the Reparation Sisters, consented to my request for an interview with her about Father Formigão. I was privileged to see his original manuscript notes, with all the questions and answers, made in 1917 as he interviewed each of the three children.

Father Formigão, who was already well known throughout Portugal at the time of the apparitions, was no believer in them at first, even though he had a deep religious devotion to Mary. He was born in Tomar on January 1, 1883, and died January 30, 1958, at Fatima. On the site of the small house in which he died now stands an apartment house built by the Blue Sisters for the care of elderly women. Sister Mary of the Incarnation proudly showed me the very spot where Father Formigão died—it is now the corner of the lobby of the hospice. She told me that she had been present with Father Formigão at the time of his death; he had held in one hand the small crucifix that had previously always stood on his desk, and in the other hand a small statue of Our Lady of Fatima.

There are many religious houses in Fatima today, but the religious community founded by Father Formigão was the first.

Father Formigão first ventured into the Cova da Iria on September 13, 1917. It seems doubtless that he had been initially alerted to the happenings in Fatima by the Lisbon newspaper reports. Then, having received news of the children's imprisonment in August, as well as other information about the alleged apparitions, he decided to be present in the Cova on September 13.

When the Diocese of Leiria-Fatima was restored, Bishop Dom José nominated Father Formigão to be a member of the diocese's Canonical Commission, and thus it came about that the latter was officially entrusted to study the "happenings" in Fatima.

As doctor of theology and as a licensed lawyer, Father Formigão was well prepared for his task. The kidnapping of the children by the administrator of Ourém in August had caused an extraordinary reaction of anger and aversion throughout Portugal. It also increased people's curiosity and the desire to be present in the Cova the following month, on September 13.

The events of September 13th must have left a strong impression on the spirit of Father Formigão, for he afterward wrote: "I resolved to return to Fatima to get to know personally and question in depth the seers [that is, the three children] and hear from them trustworthy and truthful facts of the amazing episodes that had taken place during the five preceding months."

He returned to Fatima on September 27, arriving at three o'clock in the afternoon, and went directly to Aljustrel. At the homes of the children, he conducted his first interviews: first with Francisco, next with Jacinta, and finally with Lucia when she had returned from the vintage. At that time, he formed a favorable impression; being a cautious theologian, he did not come to any definite conclusion about the "supernaturality" of the facts, but the sincerity of the seers made an indelible impression on him:

"The depositions of the children," he wrote, "are imperfect and deficient. ... But notwithstanding these imperfections—absolutely impossible to avoid in the indicated circumstances—the declarations of the humble shepherds, made on this day, ... were enough in themselves to dissipate even in more learned and more exacting souls any suspicion or apprehension about their sincerity."

Father Formigão was so convinced of the children's sincerity that at the end of his notes, made almost immediately after his interviews with them, he wrote the first "apologia" of Fatima. "From the answers of the children, and even more from their attitude and mode of presence in all the circumstances in which they found themselves, results a clarity that seems to exclude all doubts as to their perfect and absolute sincerity."

The sincerity of the seers was one thing; but it was also necessary to exclude the possibility that the children were subject to the "suggestion, the hallucination, the evil influence of the devil." In a journal entry dated September 29, 1917, Father Formigão wrote: "Only one other alternative remains. Are the events of Fatima the work of God? It is too early to answer this question firmly."

When October 13, 1917, had passed, either all would be refuted as sorcery, or new, conclusive evidence might establish the *reality* of the apparitions of the Blessed Virgin.

On his third trip to Fatima, Father Formigão had reached the profound conviction that Fatima was "the place destined by the Queen of Heaven, Patroness of Portugal, for the theater of her kindness and mercy."

ii

Preparing to go to Fatima a few days before October 13th, he knew that the presence there of a multitude of pilgrims would not permit him to make his investigations easily. He left Santarém on the 10th, at about eleven o'clock in the morning, arriving at Fatima at eleven o'clock at night. The pastor, being absent, had left instructions for Father Formigão to go to the home of Manual Goncalves, in nearby Montelo. (Thus it happened that Father Formigão—in memory of the cordial hospitality—adopted the pseudonym "Visconde de Montelo.")

Father Formigão described the solar phenomenon in several passages in his writings, but most briefly in this manner: "On the 13th of October of this year, close to 60,000 persons of all classes and social conditions gathered at the site of the apparitions, attracted by the reports of the miracle discreetly announced. It was the most frightening and divinely beautiful spectacle that one could contemplate, which unfolded before the eyes of this astonished multitude. All morning it rained torrentially. The sky in all its unbounded vastness was covered with black, dense clouds. At noon the sun suddenly broke through the clouds that covered it and, like an astonishing wheel of fire, whirled around its 'axle' for about 10 minutes, projecting in continuous explosions faggots of light and torrents of the most beautiful and variegated colors of flames."

But one circumstance moderated the enthusiasm of Dr. Formigão, as of other reflective, educated persons: Lucia had announced that the war was going to end on that day—"today"—and it did not. Father Formigão had been among those in the tumult who, moments after the phenomenon of the spinning of the sun, approached Lucia to ask her once more if the war was indeed going to end that day.

At the home of the Martos, where Lucia was also present later that evening on October 13, 1917, it was about seven o'clock when Father Formigão interviewed each of the children. It was, he knew, not the best time for such interviews. The children were exhausted, excited, and already fed up with people's questions. Their privacy had been trampled on with little concern for their feelings. But he did not want to lose the chance to talk to them within a few hours after the apparitions.

Afterward, he drew one of the first word-pictures of the seers.

> *The little one [Jacinta] did not want to come to me without her cousin (they are inseparable). Very little, very shy, she finally came to me. I was sitting. To appreciate her better, I put her on a chest and was able to observe her at will. The pastor had told me she was an angel. I wanted to see for myself. I am now convinced she is an angel with much, much love! A large, flowered handkerchief was wrapped around her head. The handkerchief was old and ragged. She had on a vest which was not very clean, and a wide skirt, which was the custom at that time. Here you have a description of how our little angel was dressed. I would like to describe her little face to you; I do not believe I will succeed, but I will at least approximate. The handkerchief, in the way she wore it, made her features even more outstanding, her lively and charming black eyes, an angelic expression revealing her captivating kindness. Very shy. I had difficulty hearing the little one's answers to my questions.*
>
> *Francisco arrived. His cap rammed over his ears, he wore a short vest; his shirt could be seen under his waistcoat; his trousers were tight-fitting. He looked like a small man. A beautiful-faced boy—bright eyes, roguish face. He had a relaxed air about him as he answered my questions.*
>
> *A little later, Lucia arrived. You can't imagine how happy Jacinta was to see Lucia. She was all smiles, ran to her, and never let go of her. It was a beautiful picture, Lucia in the center, Francisco on one side, very close to her, her head actually on top of her Jacinta. Lucia does not have features that impress one. Only her facial expression is lively. Her features are coarse—typical of the region. At first also reserved, she shortly warmed up to me.*
>
> *Notwithstanding Lucia's unattractive features, she captivates me. She has something—I don't know what—that enchants one.*

After his first visit with the three children on September 27, he had written these impressions:

The first child came. She is called Jacinta of Jesus, seven years old, pretty tall for her age, slender but not thin, her face well proportioned, dark brown complexion, dressed modestly, her skirt down to her ankles. Her appearance is that of a healthy child. Revealing perfect normalcy in her physical and moral aspect. Surprised by the presence of strange persons who came with me, which she did not expect, at first she showed great embarrassment, responding to my questions in monosyllables and in a tone of voice almost inaudible.

Moments later, her brother entered. A boy of nine years of age, who entered the room with a certain forwardness, keeping his hat on his head—most likely because he forgot to take it off. His sister signaled to him to remove it, but he did not notice. I invited him to sit on the chair next to me; he obeyed immediately without hesitation.

Lucia of Jesus appears, taller and more nourished than the other two children, lighter complexioned, robust, healthy. She presents herself to me with an ease which singularly contrasts with the excessive shyness and timidity of Jacinta. Dressed simply, her attitude does not show bashfulness and her face does not denote shyness. Her face does not reflect vanity, much less embarrassment. These exterior features must be completed with some interior characteristics which I could perceive. Even in pictures, we note the shyness and bashfulness of Jacinta, her air of innocence and kindness, her extraordinary liveliness in her movements, but also her invincible difficulty to speak.

In Francisco we note his naturalness, his manly aspect; in small points he manifests curiosity in everything that attracts his attention.

In Lucia, we note her manner in always enchanting people, her sincerity, her lack of timidity even in difficult situations.

Dr. Formigão, by frequent and close contact with the three children, won their total confidence and thus formed his opinion of their psychologies. By the end of September 1917, he had begun his defense, and eventually he would be asked to present an official report for the "canonical process" in early 1930. In his report one can see not only the results of his careful and exact study of the children, but that the children likewise came to understand well this priest from Santarém, who visited them every so often, and questioned them so lovingly, at times so seriously, but without imposing on them, without frightening them, and without forcing their replies.

iii

Francisco was the first to die. He became ill toward the end of October 1918, and the influenza consuming him eventually caused his death—the following April 4. Father Formigão recorded the circumstances of Francisco's holy death and left us a beautiful testimony. Visiting Aljustrel in 1920, he gathered the painful memories of the previous year from Francisco's mother. His manuscript notes, written in pencil, caught the natural simplicity of the boy:

" 'O godmother, give me your blessing and forgive me.' His godmother embraced him, did not want to believe he would die yet. She would say, 'O Francisco, you are not going to die yet.' Ten minutes later he passed away with a smile on his face.

"Jacinta said: 'Why are you crying? He is smiling.' She was asked: 'Why are you not crying?' Jacinta never cried, did not feel sorry for him; or, if she did, she did not show it. Not even at the funeral. She would say: 'You are the ones who will die. He didn't die; yes, he died, but he went to heaven.' But she would pray for his soul with the family."

Father Formigão also recorded the comments of Francisco's mother, Olimpia, whom he questioned on September 28, 1923, about Francisco's death: "Francisco knew he was going to die shortly," she said. "Before he died, he said: 'O my mother, look at the beautiful light there at our window.' A little later he said that it was gone. He smiled and breathed his last."

Father Formigão's relationship was more personal with Jacinta, and more important for the course of his life. Before he had finished his official interrogations of the children, he learned that Jacinta had become very ill on October 13, 1919. "After the death of Francisco, Jacinta came to visit me with her mother. The little one is like a skeleton. Her arms are frighteningly thin. Ever since she came home from the hospital in Vila Nova de Ourém, where she had been taken for two months' treatment, without results, she has a fever. Her appearance inspires compassion. Poor child, last year she was full of life and health, and today she is like a withered flower at the edge of the grave, after an attack of bronchial-pneumonia and pleurisy. Maybe an appropriate treatment in a good sanitorium might save her. Bernadette, the young lass of Lourdes, hears our Lady say: 'I will not promise you happiness in this world, but in heaven.' Could the Blessed Virgin have made an identical promise to the shepherdess of the Serra D'Aire, to whom she communicated a secret that the little one could not tell anyone? The suffering of Jacinta of Jesus was endured with Christian resignation—a font of merit that will turn her crown in heaven more brilliant and precious. Jacinta continued in this lamentable state the rest of 1919. . . ."

During Jacinta's hospitalization in Lisbon, Father Formigão had no opportunity to see her from January 21 to February 20, 1920, the day she died. For her part, Jacinta had a strong desire to see and talk to this good priest, and to communicate to him "a secret from our Lady," one that was to transform his life.

After the death of Francisco and Jacinta, he devoted his attention to Lucia. She had endured the deaths of her cousins and of her father, as well as the grave illness of her mother, who the family thought would surely die. All this stress caused Lucia to lose much weight; her health became endangered. At the same time, people with good intentions arranged visits with various good-hearted souls in order to distract her.

In the spring of 1920, Lucia took the first of a series of trips to various places near Fatima. She received attention, was fondled, and was the focus of needless publicity. This strange atmosphere disturbed her.

Before her death, Jacinta had been preoccupied with a concern that Lucia be allowed to live a life of holiness, and even sent her warnings through Father Formigão. The priest saw that it was important to safeguard Lucia's future, lest the pitiful cases of the seers of LaSalette be her lot also. When Lucia returned to Aljustrel on August 12, 1920, he persuaded Bishop Dom Jose to send Lucia to the Asilo de Vilar, a convent-school in Porto, on June 13, 1921.

Father Formigão thereafter had few opportunities to interview Lucia. On July 8, 1924, he did visit with her in Vilar; and he was present also at the ceremonies of her religious profession in Tuy, Spain, on October 3, 1928. Their conversation on the eve of her first profession of vows left Father Formigão with a longing for heaven.

In October 1939, he published an article in the Portuguese magazine *Stella*:

It is the year 1928. Just 10 years ago, in the novitiate of the Religious of St. Dorothy in Tuy, Lucia of Jesus, the leading personality of the apparitions of Fatima, was about to ascend the steps of the altar to make her total consecration to the service of God as a religious.

It was October 2, the feast of the Guardian Angel and vigil of the feast of St. Theresa of the Child Jesus.

On this day, the eve of her voluntary immolation, through special permission of the Mother Superior, I was permitted to interview, for a good length of time, the happy privileged of the Queen of Heaven.

Sister Lucia appeared in my presence, as I had expected, full of simplicity and modesty, with the same air of angelic sincerity that most of all enchanted me when, in the past, I saw her in Fatima and spoke with her on the commemorative days of the apparitions.

"Now, Sister Lucia," I asked her, "are you satisfied and are you happy that you embraced the religious life?"

"Very satisfied and happy. I have no fascination for the world with its illusions and vanities. I want to be far from it, to love and serve God more perfectly."

"Did our Lady appear to you and make revelations to you after 1917?"

"It is true. She appeared to me once during my novitiate."

"What did she tell you? Did she communicate to you something new that you would be permitted to reveal?"

"Yes. She revealed to me and recommended the devotion of the five First Saturdays."

"And what kind of devotion is this?"

"I will explain. Our Lady said: her Divine Son was very much displeased with the offenses committed against her, and especially because of the

blasphemies against her Immaculate Conception." Then she added: "Many persons have already been lost because of this, but many others would be saved if good and generous souls could be found who would make reparation for these offenses with their prayers and good works, appeasing Divine Justice in this way."

"Is the manner in which to make such reparation the practice of the devotion of the five First Saturdays?"

"Exactly. The Blessed Virgin taught me what this devotion consists of. The persons who want to practice it must go to confession, receive Holy Communion, say the Rosary, and spend 15 minutes in the company of our Lady. It is necessary to meditate on the mysteries of the Rosary. All these acts must be fulfilled with the intention to make reparation for the offenses committed against our Heavenly Mother."

"Is it indispensable that these acts be put into practice on the first Saturday of the month?"

"Because in the novitiate the day scheduled for confession was not on Saturday, I asked our Lady if it was valid to go to confession on another day. She responded affirmatively and added it could be done after the first Saturday, as long as Holy Communion is received in the state of grace."

"What did our Lady promise to persons who practice this devotion?"

"She promised she would grant many graces during their life and the grace of final perseverance."

The interview ended there.

As I prepared to leave, she asked me to spread, wherever I possibly can, the devotion to the Immaculate Heart of Mary, which I promised to do.

iv

When I spoke with Sister Mary of the Incarnation, vicar general of the Reparation Sisters, I asked especially about her memories of Father Formigão:

"Sister, who founded your religious community?"

"Dr. Manuel Nunes Formigão. He worked with young people, having founded two youth organizations. Consequently, in recognition of his work, he was given the title 'Conego' [Canon]. He was a theological advisor to the Cardinal Patriarch of Lisbon."

"When did Father Formigão found your community?"

"It was January 6, 1926. Father Formigão was born January 1, 1883, and he died January 30, 1958. He was 43 years old at the time of the founding of the community."

"Is it true that at first Father Formigão was devoted to Our Lady of Lourdes?"

"Yes. Once, when he was coming from Rome, he passed through Lourdes. There in the prayerful atmosphere and spirituality of Lourdes, he made a promise to our Lady that he would spend his life spreading devotion to her."

"How did he come to switch his devotion from Our Lady of Lourdes to Our Lady of Fatima?"

"He came to Portugal with the intention to spread devotion to Our Lady of Lourdes. In the meantime, there was a revolution here in Portugal. He had wanted to organize pilgrimages to Lourdes and spread her devotion in that way. The revolution erupted, so people could not go out of the country to Lourdes.

"He was a professor in Santarém at the seminary, and also he taught at the lyceum [secondary school]. He spread his apostolate with young people in that way. This is what *you* are doing, and you will have quite a intercessor in heaven.

"In the meantime," she went on, "our Lady appeared here in Fatima on May 13, 1917. When our Lady was appearing here, Father Formigão was still in Lisbon. Then in June, July, and August, she again appeared; but he could not be convinced that these apparitions were authentic because, not too long before, our Lady had appeared in Lourdes with her messages—and to him, the apparitions were 'completed.'

"He asked permission from the Cardinal of Lisbon to come to Fatima for the September 13th apparition. He had asked permission, because priests were not permitted to come. The Church, being prudent, did not want priests to come to Fatima. Dr. Formigão wanted to come because he was going to write in all the newspapers to inform people that the events going on at Fatima were not of supernatural origin.

"He came to Fatima with another professor. When they arrived, on September 13, there were many people here [in the Cova] already, and also the three children. Lucia was praying the Rosary. Father Formigão took up a position where the big tree now stands in the Cova [that is, the one under which the children sat awaiting the arrival of the Blessed Mother, signified by a flash of light]. The other priest took up a position on the other side of the little holm-oak tree [on which the Blessed Mother reportedly would appear]. Then Lucia said, 'There she goes. . . .'

"Father Formigão stayed on his knees afterward. The other priest came over to him and noticed that he was still kneeling with his eyes closed. He tapped him on the shoulder, and Father Formigão opened his eyes and said to the other priest, 'This is truly from heaven.' "

"What happened on September 13 that Father Formigão knew it was truly from heaven?"

"It was just the surroundings. The children were so simple, so sincere, that one could not help but conclude that they would not deceive anyone. When that priest came and found Father Formigão still on his knees and heard him say, 'This is from heaven,' he asked another priest, 'What do you think?' The other priest answered, 'I agree.'

"Father Formigão stayed on in Fatima until late afternoon, when all others had gone. Then he went to the home of the children and questioned them. He separated the children so that they could not hear each other being questioned. I have all of Father Formigão's notes he made of the questions and answers, here at our motherhouse. I will get them for you if you care to see them."

Having already read in various accounts the priest's detailed questions and the children's answers, and knowing how important they have been in leading to the Church's approval of the apparitions at Fatima, I was glad for the chance to see the manuscripts. As I looked through the original pages, in Father Formigão's own handwriting, I found each section carefully dated; so I looked especially at the entry dated October 13, 1917, the day of the "miracle of the sun."

Sister Mary of the Incarnation continued:

"Dr. Formigão asked the same questions of each of them, as one would ask a child. And on everything of importance that our Lady had said, they all agreed. About little things, like whether she wore shoes, they disagreed."

"Did our Lady ever mention Father Formigão to Jacinta?"

"Yes. Both Jacinta and Francisco contracted influenza in 1918, and Francisco became very ill. Jacinta was taken to the hospital in Vila Nova de Ourém. There were many other people ill. [The epidemic was world-wide. So many died in the Fatima area that the ringing of the church bells at each death was discontinued so as not to add to the people's fears.]

"Because they could do nothing to help Jacinta [at the hospital], they brought her home. She developed open sores in her side, and Father Formigão persuaded the parents to allow Jacinta to be taken to the Lisbon hospital. When she was taken to Lisbon, there was at first no place for her in the hospital, so she stayed for a time in an orphanage of Mother Godinho. Later she was transferred to the hospital. They treated her there. . . . Jacinta told Mother Godinho to ask Father Formigão to come to Lisbon because she had a message for him from our Lady. Father Formigão did not go immediately because of the revolution, which was anti-clerical. He thought he would wait until he could go to Lisbon on other business and then visit Jacinta. In the meantime, Jacinta died.

"Because Father Formigão did not come to visit her, Jacinta told Mother Godinho to give him this message: 'Our Lord is very much offended, and it is necessary that reparation be made. Many souls are needed to make reparation.' If there was anything more that was told to Father Formigão, he never spoke about it; but we do know that Jacinta had said that it was "our Lady's message" and was to be transmitted to Father Formigão.

"Needless to say, Father Formigão was very disturbed that he did not go to see Jacinta. For perhaps if he had, Jacinta would have told him personally what our Lady had said."

"Was it part of the message from Jacinta that our Lady wanted Father Formigão to found your religious community?"

"After receiving Jacinta's message, he started to think very seriously what this message really meant. Since our Lady had already asked here at Fatima for prayer and reparation, he thought there should be at least a group of people who would pray and make reparation to our Lord for all the offenses committed against Him. He thought that the best way to answer our Lady's request was to found a congregation dedicated to prayer and reparation, because if it would depend on the parishes, it would be only a temporary thing; and besides, there are many priests and bishops who still do not believe in the apparitions. Therefore, Father Formigão concluded that the answer was the founding of a congregation of religious for the purpose of prayer and reparation."

"In how many places are your Sisters located?"

"We have one house in the Diocese of Leiria-Fatima; four in Porto; one in Braga. There are two in the Diocese of Guarda and two in Germany. There are eleven in all, including the motherhouse here in Fatima. The Congregation was founded in Lisbon and was transferred to Fatima in 1934."

"How many Sisters are now in your Congregation?"

"There are 113. Eight sisters have already died. One postulant, three novices; and there is also a group of four who have recently asked for admission."

"Could you briefly describe your apostolate?"

"Reparation to the Eucharistic Heart of Jesus and reparation to the Immaculate Heart of Mary. These two are intertwined. There is reparation to Christ as God. The Heart of Jesus is the symbol of the offense to God. The Immaculate Heart of Mary, as a Mother, suffers because her Son is being offended, and therefore reparation must be made to her also.

"We have three vows: poverty, chastity, and obedience; but also the solemn promise to offer all our actions in reparation during our lifetime. These vows and this promise we make at our profession. Therefore, since our lives are a continuous act of reparation, we accept everything that God sends us without complaint, in the spirit of reparation.

"We also have the Eucharistic Adoration night and day here at Fatima. We have adoration at the motherhouse until noon, but continuously, day and night, in the Cova Sanctuary.

"Father Formigão thought that at least this group of souls will live the spirit of reparation that our Lady had requested. We do have some form of Eucharistic reparation in all our houses; but day and night only at the Cova Sanctuary."

"How do you support yourselves?"

"Mostly by the work of the Sisters. We do some social work. We never have had donations on a large scale, but a few years ago one of the Sisters explained our work to an American writer, and he went back to the States and wrote in a magazine about the work of the Sisters and who they were. The Congregation received quite a few donations as a result."

"Are you still in need?"

"We are not financially solvent because of our recent construction [the expansion of the hospice for aged women]. At first we had only a small house. We gradually added on. The elderly ladies we accept here pay a small fee."

"What kind of social work do you engage in besides tending to elderly women?"

"We teach in grade schools and religion programs, and work in Catholic Action wherever possible. We publish a bi-monthly magazine, *Stella*, founded by Father Formigão in 1937. I worked on *Stella* when I first entered the Congregation at age 15. We publish also the *Almanac of Our Lady of Fatima*. We try to expand the good works of the press. Through our publications, we try to spread the message of Christ. Through all our contacts, we work in the spirit of reparation."

"What do you require of girls who are interested in joining your Congregation?"

"We take girls at 18 years of age. We will take Americans. They may write us for further information."†

"Another priest besides Father Formigão who had been present at the September 13 apparition—he was a seminarian at the time—described Father Formigão to me as the 'soul of Fatima.' What do you think he meant?"

"Yes, Father Formigão is the 'soul of Fatima,' because ever since that September 13, when he felt that our Lady was really appearing, his whole life was devoted to spreading the message of Fatima. In his writings, his books, in pilgrimages he brought to Fatima, in everything he did, he did it with interest in spreading our Lady's messages. Cana Barthas, a writer, has said, 'Father Formigão was the fourth seer at Fatima. When Father Formigão would lead pilgrimages to Fatima, people would ask, has that holy priest passed by yet?'

"Instead of using the press to tell people that Fatima was a hoax (as was his original intention) or a lie, he wrote a series in the newspapers telling people that the apparitions are true.

"The ideas that he had for Lourdes, he brought to Fatima. He organized the volunteer workers at Fatima. The publication *The Voice of Fatima* was also his idea. The blessing of the sick, the processions, and so on."

"Did Father Formigão originate the processions with the miraculous statue?"

"I do not know whether the procession with the statue was his idea; but he was so humble, the type who would gently suggest an idea and not take credit if it was carried out. The procession with the statue was not organized until after the statue was made. After the Capelinha was dynamited [1922], the statue was kept by a family living in Moita and was brought to the Cova only for the 13th, until they made sure it was safe to leave it here."

"Did he continue with his youth work after he got involved in Fatima?"

"Yes, until the Congregation was founded, he did continue his works in Santerém. After he founded the Congregation, he spent most of his time in

---

†Irma Maria da Encarnaçao Vieria Esteves, Casa de Na Sa das Dores, Rua Francisco Marto 129, Apartado 20, 2495 Fatima, Portugal.

Fatima. At times he would go to Bragança for youth work. He was rector at the seminary there."

"How many years did you know Father Formigão?"

"I knew him from 1938 until 1958, when he died."

"Describe him as you remember him."

"My idea of him is that he was very humble, very delicate, a very human person. When I was a little girl, he came to my parish for Holy Week. I was standing at the foot of the stairs to the church; and as I saw this priest going into the church, for what reason I don't know, I was like a paralyzed person until he entered the church. Then, when I joined the convent years later, I found he was the same priest who had had such an effect on me."

"What was it about him that so affected you on that occasion as a little girl?"

"His attitude—the way he walked up those stairs—his stature. All had an effect on me. He possessed an attitude in which one could detect that he was in union with Christ. At the same time, he was very human and sensitive to the needs of others. He was very occupied with the well-being of others."

"Has it been suggested that his cause for beatification be introduced?"

"Yes. Father Joaquin Maria Alonso, in his book *Dr. Formigão, Man of God and Apostle of Fatima* [1979], makes that appeal. Another facet of Father Formigão is that he never gave a speech, no matter on what he spoke, without concluding with some mention of our Lady. He never stopped spreading the message of our Lady."

"Have any of your Sisters reported supernatural occurrences related to the intercession of Father Formigão since his death?"

"In the Congregation itself, we don't know of anything supernatural occurring through the intercession of Father Formigão, but people have come to us and have said that they have obtained graces through his intercession and have left a little donation in thanksgiving; but we have not looked into these yet."

"Did the perpetual adoration of the Most Blessed Sacrament in the Cova da Iria begin in 1960?"

"Yes. We have some Sisters still here who have participated from the time it began, and they still take their turns at adoration before the Blessed Sacrament."

"Did Father Formigão specifically request such perpetual adoration from members of the Congregation?"

"Yes. At the beginning we were not able to have perpetual adoration because things were not yet organized. We have felt that it was through his intercession, after his death, that we were able to begin perpetual adoration, in 1960."

"Did the opening of the 'third part' of the 'secret of Fatima' in 1960 have anything to do with your beginning perpetual adoration in that year?

"I think it had something to do with it; Bishop John Venancio gave the secret to the Cardinal Patriarch of Lisbon, and then took the secret to Rome and gave it to Pope John XXIII. When Bishop Venancio returned, I'm not sure what all went on; but right after that, Bishop Venancio gave his consent that the perpetual adoration begin immediately in the Cova.

"Dr. Formigão also intended to found a men's Order of Reparation, and even wrote up a Constitution for it. We have a copy of it, as does the bishop of Leiria; but nothing seems to come of it. When Bishop Alberto of Leiria-Fatima came to Fatima one day, I mentioned it to him, and he said, 'Yes, I have it in my mind. I'm waiting to find a good and holy priest to whom I can entrust its work.'

"Bishop Venancio wanted the perpetual adoration in the Cova because he said it was the altar of the world."

"Are you certain it was Bishop Venancio who delivered the third part of the secret to Rome?"

"Yes, definitely. . . ."

VII. *The 'Secret' of Fatima*

Having known Don João Venancio (Bishop of Fatima from 1958 to 1972) for many years, I have interviewed him on many topics; and while he was serving as international president of the Blue Army of Our Lady of Fatima, I explained for him the plans I had for my Fatima youth apostolate, the Blue Army Cadets, and received his blessing for the same. I soon came to admire his evident deep spirituality. It was he who took the "secret" of Fatima to Rome, in an envelope that he did not open. But, as he once told me, he did hold the envelope up to the sun so as to "see" the size of the paper upon which Sister Lucia had written the secret. He said he judged that Lucia's message was not a lengthy one.

i

I first interviewed Bishop Venancio formally in 1974. Since that time, Fatima has attracted increased interest in the United States and elsewhere, with even secular journals taking periodic note of the supernatural phenomena reported to have occurred at Fatima in 1917. When the "third part" of the Fatima "secret" was not publicized to the world in 1960—the year when many thought it would be revealed—a loss of interest in Fatima ensued; and some even concluded that the alleged apparitions of 1917 in Fatima were a fraud. Yet there had never been a "promise" that the third part of the Fatima secret would be revealed to the world in 1960; it was something always designated for the pope.

In 1974, I mentioned to Bishop Venancio that many priests in the United States at that time did not look favorably upon the Fatima apparitions or even the wearing of the Brown Scapular; and his reaction was this: "At St. Meinrad Seminary [in Indiana], where I spoke recently, that same opinion was put to me, and I answered that apparently they do not know the importance the Church has placed on the message of Fatima. It is most signficant that the Holy Father [Paul VI] mentioned Fatima during Vatican Council II and came to Fatima personally and presented Lucia. Before 3,000 registered journalists, before television cameras, with a gesture of his hand, the Holy Father presented Sister Lucia to the world. In this way the Pope indicated, *What she is saying is authentic. I stand behind it.*

I mentioned also that while Pope Paul VI did speak of his gift of the Golden

Rose to the Council Fathers, as a sign of the Holy See's approval of the Sanctuary of Fatima, the documents of the Council do not allude to it. Bishop Venancio replied: "It is evidently not something properly of the Council. During the most solemn part of the third session, however, before all the bishops of the world formally present, the Holy Father mentioned Fatima and spoke as head of the Church."

His view of the Fatima message was that "the most important thing you can do is to make known and to live Fatima and devotion to the Immaculate Heart of Mary and be an example to your fellow priests. Do it, live it, and preach it."

"How do I 'live' devotion to the Immaculate Heart of Mary?"

"By your evident acts of prayer, penance, reparation, and love. The best form of reparation is before and in union with the Blessed Sacrament. Fatima is reparation, reparation, reparation, reparation—and especially Eucharistic reparation."

"Are penance and reparation the same thing?"

"Yes. But there is an important distinction. The reparation requested at Fatima is often mistaken to be only reparation for personal sin. While this is not excluded, the true meaning of reparation requested at Fatima is reparation in union with Christ for the sins of the world. . . . Among the kinds of reparation, the Holy Mass is primary. Please observe that reparation is such an important part in the message of Fatima that the *intention* of reparation is essential to obtain the promise connected with the five First Saturdays."

ii

Another authority on Fatima whom I've interviewed frequently, beginning in 1974, was the late Father Joaquin Maria Alonso, C.M.F., who was appointed by the Bishop of Leiria-Fatima to prepare the definitive critical study of Fatima and its message. Father Alonso, who died in September 1981, held a doctorate in philosophy and theology from the Gregorian University in Rome and pursued further studies at Louvain, Heidelberg, and the Sorbonne. He also taught philosophy and theology in Rome, Madrid, and Lisbon. He was a member of several international Marian societies, and editor of *Ephemerides Mariologicae*, an international journal of Marian studies. He claimed to know the substance of the third part of the "secret" of Fatima.

Students of the Fatima apparitions and the messages the Virgin gave the three children commonly refer to the sum of those messages as "the secret," of which two "parts" have been publicized to the world.

The so-called first part of the Fatima secret concerns the terrible vision of hell shown the children on July 13, 1917. Our Lady then said to the children: "You have seen hell, where the souls of poor sinners go. In order to save them, God wishes to establish in the world devotion to my Immaculate Heart. If you do what I tell you, many souls will be saved, and there will be peace. The war will end; but if men do not cease offending God, another and more terrible war will break out. ...." (She was not speaking of saving souls already in hell; such are doomed forever. She spoke of saving souls on this earth, people whose lives, if not reformed, will lead them to hell.)

The second part of the Fatima secret was the desire of God that devotion be established in the world to the Immaculate Heart of Mary.

"Is it not possible," I once asked Father Alonso, "that the promise of salvation attached to making the five First Saturdays can be looked upon in a superstitious way?"

He answered: "I don't deny such a possibility, but there is no true foundation for it because it is a question concerning a devotion with a sound theological basis. Perhaps a better way to put it: there is a possibility in the abstract, but in practice it is unlikely."

"What is that theological basis?"

"It is that God wills to use the intercession of Mary, by this completely merciful means, to contribute to the application of the infinite merits of Jesus Christ, the true Savior of the world. It is our Lord who saves. God uses our Lady's intercession to obtain the application of the infinite merits of our Lord. We must never lose sight of the fact that it is our Lord who saves. It is necessary to add this last statement, because sometimes people confuse the altogether necessary saving action of Christ with the providential saving action of Mary, which is dependent on Christ. The action of Christ is necessary, but with Mary it is providential." In other words, God did not need to use Mary; yet in His providence, He has chosen to grant graces *from* his Son *through* Mary's intercession. "In Christ, it is of His right. With Mary, it is something God gives in His bounty."

"Some say Fatima is only private revelation and not public divine relation, and therefore we are free to ignore it."

"You must make a distinction. If one speaks of strict obligation in the same way that we speak of the Catholic faith, it is true that we are not strictly obliged to accept the private revelations of Fatima. But if we speak of a certain obligation to follow the Spirit, which moves the Church at every moment of time," then we are obliged to accept that in this time, "the Spirit is working in the Church through Fatima." He added that "if we want to have the sense of the Church, then the Church has approved Fatima as a great means of the Christian life. ... When I speak of the Spirit of Fatima, I speak of the Spirit who acts in a manner completely ecclesial, and for that reason altogether certain, where there is no danger for the faith and for discipline."

On another occasion (July 31, 1980), I asked Father Alonso about the "secret" of Fatima, partly because he had recently written a small book on that subject. I began by recalling that he had once said to me that Fatima is "the mind of the Church"—a phrase to which he immediately objected: "I did not say it that way. It is better to say: 'Fatima is in accord with the mind of the Church.' There are the documents of the Church, there is the Magisterium, there are all the bishops of Portugal, and there are the visits of many, many cardinals who come here. If Fatima was not in accord with the Church, these visits would not happen. Above all, there was the visit of Pope Paul VI to Fatima and his encyclical *Signum Magnum*—also the Golden Rose he gave to Fatima during the Second Vatican Council."

"Do you conjecture that the third part of the 'secret' of Fatima may be related to the crisis in the Catholic faith experienced in most of the world today?"

"Yes."

"Do you personally feel certain about that?"

"Yes. Not only probably, but definitely."

"Then you are saying that you know the full 'secret' of Fatima?"

"That is not a fair deduction. I know the secret of Fatima *indirectly*. I will give you an example of what I mean. If I see the shadow and I don't see the person, but I see from the shadow that the person has a long nose or a crooked nose, I recognize who the person is. I could see that this is the shadow of Mr. So-and-so. I know whether the Fatima secret is long or short. It is very, very short. I could also say that it cannot contain some of the things that various books claim for it. I could say it does not treat of any new punishment. It consists only of prophecies about the new condition of the Church in the world."

"You must admit," I said to him, "that if you saw the shadow of a man who had a certain type of nose, a certain shape body—say, very heavy—yet it would be possible that you would say it was Mr. So-and-so and still be mistaken."

"This is always possible, but I put it to myself as impossible."

"So what you are saying is that you indirectly know that the third part of the Fatima secret has something to do with the crisis of faith in the Church today?"

"Not only am *I* saying that, but all who know how to read can see for themselves. There are two parts of the secret already known. The third part forms a unity with the other two parts. To understand it, it must be understood in relation to the first two parts; and therefore I make an interpretation that scholars today call 'structural.' "

"Would you explain what you mean by 'structural'?"

" 'Structural' is a very common word, here used in a very specialized sense. It signifies that everything must be understood *in conjuction with* all that surrounds it. It is the same, in a biblical context, as exegesis.' "

"But still you don't know *exactly* what the third part of the Fatima secret is, but only generally?"

"Specifically, I do not know. When I started to investigate and write about Fatima, the text of the third part of the secret was already in the Vatican archives; and I cannot say what the exact text is."

"In your book *The Secret of Fatima; Fact and Legend*, you indicate that everything has already been revealed about Fatima."

"Yes. You should not expect any more revelation on Fatima."

Father Alonso told me that, as the designated official historian of the Fatima apparitions, he has copies and photocopies of all the documents, including personal letters, related to them.

iii

It was in late 1943 or early 1944 when Sister Lucia wrote down the third part of the secret, in the form of a letter, under the insistence of the Bishop of Leiria-Fatima. The contents of the sealed letter were known only to Lucia, and she gave instruction that it was to be opened "not before 1960," or after her death. The Bishop of Leiria-Fatima at first kept it in a safe until it was removed to the Vatican. No copy of Lucia's original exists.

Years before 1960 arrived, the letter became the object of world-wide curiosity. The fact that it was known that our Lady had foretold the end of World War I and the coming of World War II, led some to spread sensational speculations or apocalyptic pronouncements as to what the letter contained.

In 1960, Pope John XXIII opened the letter and showed it to a few close aides. He then ordered it returned to the Vatican archives; its contents have not been revealed to the world. A reliable source in Fatima told me that shortly after his election (June 21, 1963), Pope Paul VI also read the letter.

Those who had built up an anticipation that the letter would be published were disappointed when it was not. Sensationalizing led to a rumor that Pope John had not dared to reveal the letter's contents because its message was so terrifying. At the opposite extreme were those who said it was not published because it was not worth revealing.

The saddest result of the sensationalism and excessive curiosity was that many people began to forget about the *known* parts of our Lady's message. St. Bernadette of Lourdes had been given a "secret" by our Lady, too. She went to her death with it. What was needed in the case of Fatima was a study of the Fatima message in its entirety, as revealed to the world and in relation to the entirety of Catholic faith. As Father Alonso points out, Fatima is not a theological novelty, "an interpolation introduced into the deposit of faith." The third part of the secret will not contain "a new doctrine, something original which has come to revolutionize dogma, morals, or Christian spirituality."

In 1976, Father Alonso wrote: "My primary intention is twofold. I want first to do away, once and for all, with the mystifications, the caricatures, the hair-raising exaggerations, the cheap and sensational apocalyptic writings which have been produced on the subject of Fatima and its Secret. ... Although in no way meant to fill us with fear and dread, Fatima and its Secret do present us with something deeply serious, for they bring us face to face with the mysteries of eternal life."

When the canonical investigation of Fatima was completed and the Bishop of Leiria-Fatima declared (May 13, 1930) that the Fatima apparitions could be held to be of supernatural origin, the apparitions of the Angel of Peace were still unknown to the public. It was not until May 1942 that the Cardinal of Lisbon revealed them. Already in 1917, Lucia had been prohibited by her spiritual directors from speaking of the angelic apparitions so that our Lady's message would be "accepted" more readily.

Our Lady had not specifically told the children at the May apparition to keep silence about the reparation to her Immaculate Heart and the promise that they would go to heaven; the children simply felt an impulse not to speak of those things at the time. The apparitions of the Virgin in June and July motivated the children all the more not to speak of reparation to the Heart of Mary. They felt that that subject was so closely connected with the real "secret" (that is, the "third part"), that to mention it would be to disclose the secret.

Lucia's memoirs drew a close connection between the mystery of hell and devotion to the Immaculate Heart of Mary: calling upon the intercession of our Lady, through devotion to her Immaculate Heart, would save souls who would otherwise be lost.

When Lucia was later questioned about the terrible war she had predicted would break out during the reign of Pope Pius XI, her questioners pointed out that World War II did not begin till the pontificate of Pope Pius XII; Lucia answered that the war had already begun earlier when Nazi Germany annexed Austria (March 1938; Pius XI died February 10, 1939). She had written also about a "sign" that our Lady had told the children would presage the war: "When you see a night lit up by an unknown light, know that it is the sign God gives you that he is about to punish the world for its crimes by means of war, hunger, and persecution of the Church and the Holy Father." Lucia recognized that sign in the prominent aurora borealis of early 1938, which she has always held was not a natural phenomenon. She has also said that the war, which "officially" began in September 1939, could have been prevented if there had taken place the Communion of reparation on the five First Saturdays and the consecration of Russia to the Immaculate Heart.

In November 1981, the bishops of the United States voted to petition the Holy Father for the *collegial* consecration of Russia to the Immaculate Heart. Sister Lucia had indicated that our Lord desired such a collegial consecration to be made, so it would be manifest to the world that the conversion of Russia was the fruit of the intercession of the Virgin Mary. In May 1982, Pope John Paul II went to Fatima, in prayerful thanksgiving for his having survived an assassin's attempt on his life a year earlier; and during that visit, he made the collegial consecration that Lucia had asked for.

We would seem to be living in an intermediate period of purification for ourselves, the Church, and the world. According to the Fatima revelation, the triumph of the Immaculate Heart of Mary, ushering in the social reign of the Sacred Heart of Jesus, will come, when "a period of peace will be granted to the world." First there was needed the consecration of Russia to Mary; its eventual conversion would bring the benefits of peace to the world. Penance—especially reparation through the devotion of the five First Saturdays—is required to bring about that conversion.

Francisco and Jacinta had been cautioned by Lucia not to speak of reparation to the Immaculate Heart, lest others discover the "secret." The administrator (mayor) of Vila Nova de Ourém, Arturo de Oliveira Santos, who had held the three children for three days in Ourém, thought that the "secret" contained the whole mystery of the supposedly marvelous happenings in the Cova. Lucia was therefore always hesitant to tell or write about reparation to the Immaculate Heart. At the end of 1935, when she was ordered by the bishop of Fatima to write down all her recollections concerning Jacinta, she had the same worry; for how could she write about Jacinta's interior life, which was so closely connected to devotion to the Immaculate Heart, without giving away the "secret" the children had received on July 13, 1917?

In her third *Memoir* (August 1941), Lucia, now convinced she was permitted to reveal the first "two parts" of the secret, wrote of it out of obedience to the bishop's renewed request:

> ... *I have given thought to the matter and decided that, as God was speaking to me through you, the moment had arrived to reply to two questions which have often been sent to me, but which I have put off answering until now....*
>
> *This will entail my speaking about the Secret, and thus answering the first question.*
>
> *What is the Secret?*
>
> *It seems to me that I can reveal it, since I already have permission from heaven to do so. God's representatives on earth have authorized me to do this several times and in various letters, one of which, I believe, is in your keeping. This letter is from Father Jose Bernardo Gonsalves, and in it he advises me to write to the Holy Father, suggesting, among other things, that I should reveal the Secret.*

Father Alonso noted that "the fourth *Memoir*, written in December 1941, repeats the same text about the July Secret as in the third *Memoir*, except that it adds this phrase: 'In Portugal, the dogma of the faith will always be preserved: etc. ...' (*sic*). Within this section marked by dots was the third part of the Secret." Lucia had written down the first two parts in 1941. When she fell seriously ill in mid-1943, the bishop of Leiria-Fatima asked her to write down the remainder of the secret. Because of the graveness of her illness—beginning in June 1943—the bishop feared she would leave this world and take the third part of the secret with her. It was in the midst of her painful sickness that Lucia wrote down the third part, in obedience to the bishop's command.

Though she was always obedient, Lucia nonetheless found it difficult to carry out that command. She tried several times to put what he asked for in writing, without success. Finally, by January 9, 1944, she succeeded. She wrote it on a sheet of paper, placed it inside an envelope, and sealed the envelope. When the bishop received the sealed envelope, he placed it into another, larger envelope, sealed it, and wrote upon it in his own hand:

> *This envelope with its contents is to be given to His Eminence Cardinal Dom Manuel, Patriarch of Lisbon, after my death.*
>
>
>
> *Leiria, December 8, 1945*
>
> ✠ *Jose, Bishop of Leiria.*
>
>

Sister Lucia had asked him to keep the letter in his own possession until his death, when it should be given to the patriarch. There was also an agreement between them that the document "would not be opened before 1960, or only after Lucia's death."   The second bishop of Leiria-Fatima, John Venancio, told me that when the sealed envelope passed to him, he could have opened it, but did not. Nor had his predecessor opened it. Canon Galamba once asked the latter why he never opened it, and received this answer: "It is not my duty to interfere in this matter. Heaven's secrets are not for me, nor do I need to burden myself with this responsibility."

Cardinal Cerejeira of Lisbon once spoke of the secret of Fatima as follows: "From the two parts already revealed of the so-called Secret (the third part of which has not been made known, but has been written and placed in a sealed envelope and will be opened in 1960), we know enough to enable us to conclude that the salvation of the world, in this extraordinary moment in history, has been placed by God in the Immaculate Heart of Mary."

Cardinal Alfredo Ottaviani (d. 1979) was one of the few persons permitted by Pope John XXIII to read what Lucia had written of the third part of the secret. He subsequently said to Father Alonso:

> *The Message was not to be opened before 1960. In May of 1955, I asked Lucia the reason for that date. She answered, 'Because then it will seem clearer.' This made me think that the Message was prophetic in tone, for it is precisely in prophecy, as we so often read in Sacred Scripture, that there exists a veil of mystery. . . . The envelope which contained the Secret of Fatima was received sealed by the Bishop of Leiria, and however much Lucia said that he could read it, he did not wish to do so. He wanted to respect the Secret even out of reverence for the Holy Father. He [Dom Jose] sent it to the Apostolic Nuncio, then*

Monsignor Cento (now Cardinal Cento). . . . The latter transmitted it faith-fully to the Sacred Congregation for the Doctrine of the Faith, which had asked for it, in order to prevent something of so delicate a nature, not destined to be given . . . to the public, from falling, for any reason whatsoever, even acciden-tally, into alien hands.

There had been false reports that Pope Pius XII had read the secret when it was transferred to Rome in 1957. Pius XII died on October 9, 1958. John XXIII did read the secret, as Cardinal Ottaviani recalled:

The Secret arrived in Rome and was taken to the Sacred Congregation for the Doctrine of the Faith. Still sealed, it was later, in 1960, taken to Pope John XXIII. The Pope broke the seal, and opened the envelope. Although [the letter was written] in Portuguese, he told me afterwards that he understood the text in its entirety. Then he himself placed it in another envelope, sealed it, and sent it to be placed in one of those archives that are like a well where the paper sinks deeply into the dark, black depths, and where no one can distinguish anything at all. So really, it is difficult to say where the Secret of Fatima is now. . . .

I, who have had the grace and the gift to read the text of the Secret—though I too am bound by the Secret—I can say that all that is rumored about it is sheer fantasy.

According to Father Alonso, Pope John XXIII received the document at Castel Gandolfo, saying, "I reserve the right of reading it with my confessor" (Msgr. Alfredo Cavagna):

"The letter was read a few days after being delivered to the Holy Father, but, in order to be absolutely sure about certain Portuguese expressions, the help of Msgr. Paulo Jose Tavares was sought. The contents of the document were made known to the officials of the Sacred Congregation for the Doctrine of the Faith and of the Secretariat of State, and to a few other persons. It is cer-tain that the Holy Father spoke about the matter with his close aides. How-ever, he made no public statement. He simply said, 'This makes no reference to my time,' and left final action to his successors."

In May 1960, the Cardinal of Lisbon spoke as follows: "Our Lady has al-ready drawn . . . a picture of contemporary events, with persecutions in the So-viet Union and the destruction of certain nations. At the same time she has giv-en us the remedy: the consecration of the world to her Immaculate Heart. In these apocalyptic times, it is you yourselves who have the remedy in your own hands. Many are concerned about the revelation of the third part of the Secret of Fatima. They forget, however, that the essential message has already been given, and that is what we most need to know: that we are not to offend God and that we are to live in His grace."

Lucia has always thought of the "conversion of Russia" as not limited to the return of the Russian people to orthodox Christian faith or the rejection of Marxist atheism, but rather as a total, perfect conversion to the Roman Catholic Church.

Bishop John Venancio of Leiria-Fatima once complained publicly that people were beginning to act as if the main or most important part of the Fatima message was the third part, whereas the most important part was that which was already known. Curiosity about the unknown third part of a secret was occupying the masses, and few were living the essence of the message long publicized.

It is beyond doubt true that the sensationalism of the press, the curiosity promoted by communications media concerning the Fatima secret, together with many false versions of what the secret entails, have made it difficult for the Holy See to publicize the secret at a time when many have been ready to read many false meanings into it. (A similar written "secret" associated with Our Lady of La Salette was placed in the Vatican archives about a century and a half ago, and false reports are occasionally circulated about it too.)

v

Even if the Holy See never reveals the text of the third part of the Fatima secret, its contents can be inferred.

Bishop Venancio, for example, once observed that the contents of that third part "cannot contradict what is contained in the parts of the message already known since 1942. Wherefore, if the parts of the secret already revealed cannot be in opposition to what we already know of the message, much less can they be in opposition to the gospel. The gospel tells us that God alone knows the time of the end of the world. The message of Fatima is not, therefore, a message of death, an incitement to panic and terror. It is an affirmation of life and hope."

We can remember also that regarding the general character of the undisclosed part of the Fatima message, Lucia had said it was good for some and bad for others. Once, urged on by her mother to say whether it was good or bad, she answered that it was good for whoever wished to believe.

Father Alonso has written that "the unity of the three parts which constitute the communication of July, 1917, . . . obliges us to discern clearly what is revealed and what is kept hidden, and also enables us to surmise, with reasonable probability, the nature of that which is held back. The literary structure which Lucia adopts when she begins to write is quite clear: 'Well, the Secret is made up of three distinct things, two of which I am now going to reveal.' When, therefore, there is a question of hazarding a guess about the third 'thing,' it should not be disconnected from the other two as though it were a second thought that had been overlooked."

Lucia's comment that the "dogma of faith" would be preserved in Portugal implies that other nations may experience a crisis of faith. The significance of the fact that Lucia addressed her letter to the Holy Father was weighed by Cardinal Ottaviani:

> *The world has lent an ear to Lucia's message, to that message which, over and above the parts which were private and personal, and the part which referred to the world as a whole, contained the third part of those things which our Lady had confided to her, not indeed for Lucia herself, nor for the world, at least not directly, but rather for the Vicar of Jesus Christ. . . . The Bishop [of Fatima] wished to respect the secret, also out of reverence for the Holy Father. . . . Yes, the secret is important; it is important for the Holy Father for whom it was destined. It was addressed to him. And if the one to whom it was addressed has decided not to declare 'now is the moment to make it known to the world,' we should be content with the fact that in his wisdom he wished it to remain a secret.*

What Sister Lucia has always put forward as of most importance is the *intercessory power* of the Immaculate Heart of Mary, which she calls the "sign of salvation in these latter times." Father Alonso observed: "What is always asserted is that if this powerful intercession is not put forward in the Church as it should be, the Church will find herself exposed to most serious perils that will affect even her very dogmas."

Sister Lucia complained about having to write down the third part of the message because, "in a way, I have already said it."

Her reference to the state of the faith in Portugal has been interpreted in both optimistic and pessimistic ways. Cardinal Ottaviani preferred optimism, when he spoke of Fatima fifty years after the apparitions:

> *The relationship of the message of Fatima with conditions in the Church in certain regions has become evident. In such areas, the attacks against religion are causing them to feel the weight of persecution. There, too, the message of hope and conversion exists, even before it becomes common knowledge, and this conversion can be hastened by the prayers of all who are devoted to Our Lady of Fatima. . . . There are already signs which give us a glimpse of new situations which are beginning to appear. I may perhaps be optimistic, but it seems to me that the Holy Virgin is encouraging us to have confidence. These revealing signs are various indications of developments in certain countries, and of success in an ecumenism which is bringing peoples more closely together, even those who are not Catholic, but who glory, and justly so, in the name of Christian. Then there are signs of all the Holy Father's initiatives in favor of peace. . . . These are all signs which lead us to hope that . . . our Lady wishes to give us*

a sign of her satisfaction with her children, to give new hope to the Christian world. We must say then: let us welcome our Lady's desire, and let us hasten its fulfillment by prayer.

Finally, we should note the careful analysis by Father Alonso, who, next to Sister Lucia, was, until his recent death, the foremost living authority on Fatima. His comments on the importance of the third part of the secret (or message) that our Lady gave the children at the June 13 apparition may stand as the best available opinion on a complicated and controversial subject:

In the period preceding the great triumph of the Immaculate Heart of Mary, tremendous things are to happen. These form the content of the third part of the Secret. What are they?

If in Portugal the dogma of the faith will always be preserved, it can be clearly deduced from this that in other parts of the Church these dogmas are going to become obscure or even lost altogether. It is quite possible that the message not only speaks of a "crisis of faith" in the Church during this period, but also, like the Secret of La Salette, that it makes concrete references to internal strife among Catholics and to the deficiencies even among the upper ranks of the hierarchy.

Lucia has several times spoken of the deficiencies of priests and religious. With regard to bishops, however, she gives proof of [her] exquisite delicacy, saying for example: "On account of all the sacrifice and effort of the bishops for the promotion of the cult and glory of the Immaculate Heart of Mary, and because they directly represent our Lord, I have for all of them a great esteem, love, and veneration."

When, therefore, Sister Lucia has some "communication" from heaven for bishops, as for example for those in Spain, it cannot be regarded as a "charismatic excess."

Can the "intermediate" period of the text be identified as the one in which we are now living? We may affirm in general that this is so, for ... the internal troubles of the post-conciliar Church bear witness to a lamentable state of affairs, clearly pointed out by Pope Paul. This has been characterized not only by conflicts and antagonisms within the Church, but also by tremendous weakening in theological teaching and an excessively critical spirit that has undermined Scriptural exegesis.

No one can doubt that this is what has happened. But is it precisely to this condition that the words of the text allude, "In Portugal, the dogma of the faith will always be preserved"? There are assuredly good grounds for believing that they do. It is not, however, easy to say if the third part of the Secret refers to the era that we are living in today or to another epoch yet to come. To limit the "intermediate" period to the present time is extremely probable, but not cer-

tain. One conclusion does indeed seem to be beyond doubt: the content of the unpublished part of the Secret does not refer to new wars or political upheavals, but to happenings of a religious and intra-Church character, which of their very nature are still more grave.

It is thus understandable that Cardinal Ottaviani should persist in saying that the Secret message was not addressed directly to the world, but to the Pope in person. Also it is easy to understand that prudence counseled the Pope not to add to the animosities within the Church between divergent tendencies and opinions. This is especially so since Fatima had come to be regarded as one of the reactionary elements of the post-conciliar Church; so much so, indeed, that Pope Paul's pilgrim-journey to Fatima [in 1967] was criticized by some as being a return to attitudes "superceded" by the Council. It is understandable also that the Secret and all its history should have been harshly criticized by the progressive element that has prevailed in certain sectors of the Church.

Moreover, how are we to understand Lucia's great difficulty in writing the final part of the Secret when she had already written other things that were extremely difficult to put down? Had it been merely a matter of prophesying new and severe punishments, Sister Lucia would not have experienced difficulties so great that a special intervention from Heaven was needed to overcome them. But if it were a matter of internal strife within the Church and of serious pastoral negligence on the part of high-ranking members of the hierarchy, we can understand how Lucia experienced a repugnance that was almost impossible to overcome by any natural means.

Still, the famous document must also contain some elements of hope ana promise provided that the Church, the hierarchy and the faithful, turn to true prayer and penance and give themselves, in confidence and love, to the Immaculate Heart of Mary.   —THE SECRET OF FATIMA (1938)

When Pope Paul VI went to Fatima for the fiftieth anniversary of the apparitions—on May 13, 1967—he spoke to the gathered throng in a way that seemed clearly to draw on his knowledge of the third part of the secret:

You all know our special intentions which have characterized this pilgrimage. Now we recall them, so that they give voice to our prayer and enlightenment to those who hear them. The first intention is for the Church; the Church, one, holy, catholic, and apostolic. We want to pray, as we have said, for its internal peace. The Ecumenical Council has revitalized the heart of the Church, has opened up new vistas in the field of doctrine, has called all her children to a greater awareness, to a more intimate collaboration, to a more fervent apostolate. We desire that these be preserved and extended. What terrible damage would be provoked by arbitrary interpretations, not authorized by the teaching of the Church, disrupting its traditional and constitutional structure, replacing

Pope John Paul II prayed at the site of the Fatima apparitions on his May 13, 1982,
pilgrimage of thanksgiving. The statue of Our Lady of Fatima
rests on a pillar near the entrance to the Capelinha. The pillar marks
the location of the small holm-oak tree above which Mary appeared to the three shepherd
children in 1917.

the theology of the true and great Fathers of the Church with new and peculiar ideologies; interpretations intent upon stripping the norms of faith of that which modern thought, often lacking rational judgment, does not understand and does not like. Such interpretations change the apostolic fervor of redeeming charity to the negative structures of a profane mentality and of worldly customs. What a delusion our efforts to arrive at universal unity would suffer, if we fail to offer to our Christian brethren, at this moment divided from us, and to the rest of humanity, which lacks our faith in its clear-cut authenticity and in its original beauty, the patrimony of truth and of charity, of which the Church is the guardian and the dispenser.

We want to ask of Mary a living Church, a true Church, a united Church, a holy Church. We want to pray together with you, in order that the aspirations and efforts of the Council may find fulfillment through the fruits of the Holy Spirit, the font of the true Christian life, whom the Church worships tomorrow on the feast of Pentecost. These fruits are enumerated by the Apostle Paul: "love, faithfulness, joy, peace, patience, kindness, goodness, gentleness and self-control." We want to pray that the love of God now and forever reign in the world; that His laws guide the conscience and customs of modern man. Faith in God is the supreme light of humanity; and this light not only must never be extinguished in the hearts of men, but must renew itself through the stimulus which comes from science and progress. This thought, which strengthens and stimulates our prayer, brings us to reflect, at this moment, on those nations in which religious liberty is almost totally suppressed; and where the denial of God is promulgated as representative of the truth of these times and the liberation of the people, whereas this is not so. We pray for such nations; we pray for the faithful of these nations, that the intimate strength of God may sustain them and that true civil liberty be conceded to them once more.

Before Pope John Paul II went to Fatima on May 13, 1982, he had previously invited the bishops of the Church to unite with him in renewing the consecration of Russia and of the world to the Immaculate Heart of Mary (apostolic letter dated April 19, 1982). At Fatima, consequently, he invoked that consecration in these words:

I am here, united with all the pastors of the Church in that particular bond whereby we constitute a body and a college, just as Christ desired the Apostles to be in union with Peter. In the bond of this union, I utter the words of the present act, in which I wish to include, once more, the hopes and anxieties of the Church in the modern world. . . . Before you, Mother of Christ, before your Immaculate Heart, I today, with the whole Church, unite myself with our Redeemer in this His consecration for the world and for people, for whom only His divine Heart has the power to obtain pardon and to secure reparation.

The power of this consecration lasts for all time and embraces all individuals, peoples, and nations. It overcomes every evil that the spirit of darkness is able to awaken, and has awakened in our times, in the heart of man in his history. . . .

How pained we are that the invitation to repentance, to conversion, and to prayer has not met with the acceptance it should have received.

Mother of the Church! Enlighten the People of God along the paths of faith, of hope, and of love! Help us to live with the whole truth of the consecration of Christ for the entire human family . . . .

Concerning the meaning of Fatima, Pope John Paul added these comments: "If the Church has accepted the message of Fatima, it is above all because that message contains a truth and a call whose basic content is the truth and the call of the gospel itself. 'Repent, and believe in the gospel' (Mark 1:15); these are the first words that the Messiah addressed to humanity. The message of Fatima is . . . a call to conversion and repentance, as in the gospel, . . . [and was] addressed particularly to this present century. The Lady of the message seems to have read with special insight the 'signs of the time,' the signs of *our* time."

VIII.   'Time Capsule of Our Future'

The May 18, 1981, English-language edition of *L'Osservatore Romano*, the Vatican newspaper, contained an article describing the Marian shrine at Fatima as a "time capsule of our future." The author—writing just after the attempted assassination of Pope John Paul II on May 13—recalled that "for months, careful and thoughtful persons had been repeating to me their fears about the risks that the Holy Father, always so exposed, might run in a world that has become more and more violent and unpredictable. It was in everyone's thoughts. ... Yesterday, Wednesday, 13 May, was the day of Our Lady of Fatima. Precisely on that day, 64 years ago, the Virgin had appeared to the three children tending sheep, at Cova da Iria, and had entrusted her messages to them. Our Lady announced serious trials for the world and for the Church, called for intense prayer, and promised that her heart would triumph.

"In the place of the apparitions," the article continued, "officially recognized by the Pastors of the Church, a shrine has arisen which, unlike all the other Marian shrines, is like *the time capsule of our future*. At Fatima, more than in any other place, Our Lady became a sharer in the history of men and peoples, involving them in the commitment for the physical and spiritual salvation of the world.

"Our Lady of Fatima has protected the Holy Father, this man so devoted to her veneration and so dedicated to the fate of the human family. She did not prevent the forces of evil, embodied in the hand of a poor young man, from hurling themselves at her faithful servant, but she saved him from death. For the believer, it is not a pious fancy. The heavenly Mother is one of the most concrete realities that John Paul II has made the Christian community perceive, confused though it sometimes is. ..."

Before *L'Osservatore Romano* had time to publish its reaction to the shooting of the Pope, the Associated Press wire service carried a news story headed "Fatima Shielded the Pope."

i

On August 12, 1981, I was privileged to stand, with approximately 100 young men, beneath the Pope's window at Gemelli Hospital in Rome. There the young men cheered, "John Paul II, we love you"—much to the pleasure of His Holiness, who smiled and threw kisses in return. The young men sang a Fatima hymn to the tune of "The Battle Hymn of the Republic."

Two days later, the Pope was released from the hospital. Before he left, he acknowledged to the patients he left behind, and to the world, that he had suffered during the months following the attack on his life. At Fatima, the Virgin Mother had said in 1917 that the Holy Father would have much to suffer if people did not repent, turn from their sins, perform Eucharistic reparation, and return to her Son, Jesus Christ. During the decades since 1917, there has been recurring speculation, with each succeeding pope, as to which pope Mary meant. As the 1980s began, a common view was that until the promised triumph of the Immaculate Heart, which would be late in coming, every pope would have much to suffer. In this connection, one might reflect on the fact that Jesus shed His blood in the Garden of Olives before a hand was laid on Him.

An Italian nun known for her personal dedication to the Immaculate Heart of Our Lady of Fatima told me that when she succeeded in visiting the Pope in Gemelli Hospital, he requested of her the published memoirs of Sister Lucia. *Memórias e Cartas da Irmã Lúcia*, the standard edition, containing the text in three languages, contains also a documentary of letters that Lucia has written over the years to spiritual advisors, to her bishop, and even to the Holy Father. The *Memoirs* thus formed part of the Pope's spiritual reading during his recuperation.

Not long before the attempted assassination on May 13, 1981, my telephone rang. "This is BBC in London calling. There has been a hijacking of an Irish jetliner with more than 100 people on board in France. An Australian, Laurence James Downey, claiming to be a former Trappist monk, demanded that the Vatican release to the world the third part of the Fatima secret. Would you agree to an interview on the Fatima message for BBC?"

"London . . . England?" I inquired.

"Yes." The caller mentioned that as I had written often about Fatima, I seemed to be the person to interview on the subject. Would I agree? Yes.

I was asked first about St. Bernadette and Our Lady of Lourdes, and then about Fatima. I thought at the time that heaven had strange ways to draw attention to the Fatima message, so long ignored. "God writes straight with crooked lines."

I was asked if it was true that the letter containing the undisclosed portion of the Fatima secret had been opened by Pope John XXIII and that he had registered shock and hid the secret in the Vatican archives, never to be revealed; and whether that Pope had subsequently discussed it with Nikita Khrushchev and John Kennedy, and so on.

The gist of my reply was that the essence of the Fatima message is not the third part of a secret: that that part was addressed specifically to the Pope, although destined for the whole world; that therefore the Pope had the prerogative not to release it to the world; that I knew of no evidence that John

XXIII had "registered shock"; that the reports about the secret and its contents being made known to Khrushchev and Kennedy are false and have been denied by high authorities associated with Fatima; that Pope Pius XII correctly described Fatima as "a reaffirmation of the Gospels"; that our Lady was a catechist at Fatima, calling the world back to prayer, to the Eucharist, to her Son of the Gospels; that surveys show that the average person, even if Catholic, does not know the Fatima message; that so much concern about the third part of a secret among those who do not even know the first two revealed parts was a bit strange; that St. Bernadette also had been given a "secret" at Lourdes but went to the grave with it; and that for anyone truly concerned about the basic message of Fatima, it is Eucharistic reparation.

The BBC interviewer mentioned that some have conjectured the secret has to do with the end of the world. "That's impossible," I replied. "The over-all message of Fatima is light and hope. Our Lady said, 'In the end, my Immaculate Heart will triumph. . . . A time of peace will be conceded to the world.' "

"You are saying, then, that the third part of the Fatima secret has to do with the breakup of the Catholic Church?"

I explained that I was not saying anything like that. Rather, I said, "individual Catholics—priests, religious, even some bishops here and there—could be disturbed in the faith, have it distorted for themselves. But the Catholic Church will never be destroyed. The universal Church of Catholicism will always endure, to the end of the world. We have Christ's promise for that."

"It appears the Fatima message is political?"

"It is not political. It is religious."

"But what about Communism, the political implications of its taking over countries? Just what is the Blue Army?"

I replied, "Our Lady spoke of the danger that the 'errors of Russia' would spread throughout the world, promoting wars and persecutions of the Church. The Communist revolution in Russia, beginning in April 1917, succeeded by November. During those six months, our Lady was appearing in Fatima, Portugal, telling three young children that those wars would spread if her wishes for mankind were not granted." I explained that the Blue Army is not a political organization but a worldwide religious effort to make the message of Fatima known. It does not advocate tanks and guns but prayer and sacrifice for the defeat of Communism. The reign we anticipate is the social reign of Jesus Christ as King.

ii

A great French author, who never visited Fatima, nonetheless penetrated the authentic signs of the events that made 1917 one of the watershed-years of the 20th century in calling them "an explosion of the supernatural" (Hilaire Belloc).

Archbishop Fulton J. Sheen saw in the Cova da Iria the "White Square," which he contrasted with the Red Square in Moscow.

In still another White Square, that of St. Peter's Basilica, while the multitude prayed and sang at Fatima, the Holy Father was struck by *three* criminal bullets. Many of the events of Fatima have occurred in threes. The angel appeared three times in 1916, preparing the three children for the coming of God's Mother. The angel, who invited the children to imitate him, prayed his various prayers three times. A pillar of bluish mist seen by people at the Cova in 1917 appeared three times. Three months before the final apparition of October 13, 1917, our Lady announced the exact day and hour when she would perform a miracle "so that all may believe." When the miracle of the spinning of the sun finally occurred, at the exact day, hour, and place announced three months in advance, it took place in three phases.

Mary's chief work at Fatima was to bring us to a response to faith in the existence of the three divine Persons—just as the angel prostrated himself to the ground and repeated three times, "Most Holy Trinity, Father, Son, and Holy Spirit, I adore you profoundly."

Cardinal Hoeffner, Archbishop of Cologne and president of the German Episcopal Conference, delivered the homily at Fatima on May 13, 1981, shortly before the Pope was struck by the three bullets:

> *During the first centuries of Christianity, innumerable martyrs died for Christ. But in all the centuries since Christ was born, no blood of martyrdom has flowed as much as it has in the 20th century, when we talk so much about progress and humanity. For two thousand years, in no other century has so much blood been poured as in our century—in two world wars, in persecution of Jews, in civil or racial wars, in waves of terror and violence all over the world. When Mary was at the foot of the cross, many inhabitants of Jerusalem must have thought: "This is the end—a catastrophe." Maybe today there are also some who might think this way: "The Church won't last much longer." As Mary is the model of the suffering and persecuted Church, so she is the model for the Church which awaits the glory of the Lord.*

In his first public address after his release from the hospital, on October 7, 1981, speaking again in St. Peter's Square, Pope John Paul II reflected on the previous five months:

> *Today it has been granted to me, after a long interruption, to resume the general audiences which have become one of the fundamental forms of pastoral service of the Bishop of Rome. The last time, the pilgrims who came to Rome gathered for such an audience on May 13th. However, it could not take place. Everyone knows why.*
>
> *Today, after an interval of five months, beginning this meeting so dear to*

me and to you, I cannot help referring to the day of May 13th. But first I can-
not but express the emotion and grief that the news of the tragic death of Egyp-
tian President Sadat caused me yesterday. . . .

During these long weeks of hospitalization at the Gemelli Polyclinic, the
episode of the most ancient days of the Church, at Jerusalem, described in the
Acts of the Apostles, often came to mind. Herod had arrested Peter: "And
when he had seized him, he put him in prison, and delivered him to four
squads of soldiers to guard him, intending after the Passover to bring him out
to the people. So Peter was kept in prison; but earnest prayer for him was
made to God by the Church. The very night when Herod was about to bring
him out, Peter was sleeping between two soldiers, bound with two chains, and
sentries before the door were guarding the prison; and behold, an angel of the
Lord appeared, and a light shone in the cell; and he struck Peter on the side
and woke him, saying, 'Get up quickly.' And the chains fell off his hands. And
the angel said to him, 'Dress yourself and put on your sandals.' And he did so.
And he said to him, 'Wrap your mantle around you and follow me.' And he
went out and followed him; he did not know that what was done by the angel
was real, but thought he was seeing a vision."

This episode . . . often came to mind during my stay in the hospital. Even if
the circumstances then and those of today seem so different, it was, however,
difficult for the convalescent who is Peter's Successor in this Roman Episcopal
See, not to meditate on these words of the Apostle: "I am sure that the Lord
has rescued me from the hand of Herod and from all that people were expect-
ing. . . ."

And again I have become indebted to the Blessed Virgin and to all the Pa-
tron Saints. Could I forget that the event in St. Peter's Square took place on
the day and at the hour when the first appearance of the Mother of Christ to
the poor little peasants has been remembered for over 60 years at Fatima in
Portugal? For, in everything that happened to me on that very day, I felt that
extraordinary motherly protection and care, which turned out to be stronger
than the deadly bullet. . . ."

As the Fatima anniversary dates of 1982 approached, there was a surge of interest when it was learned that John Paul II would go to Fatima. The hope of
millions was fulfilled by the Pope's collegial consecration on May 13, 1982.
Sister Lucia afterward confirmed that the collegial consecration the Lady had
requested had indeed taken place; but she added, "It is late, and Communism
has spread throughout the world. It will have its effect, but each of us must respond to the consecration."

iii

The papacy is very much a part of the Fatima message. The pope, chief "vicar" of Christ on earth, is the *visible* head of the universal Church, as Jesus is the

invisible Head. As the events of history unfold, one sees the meaning of the message of Fatima also gradually unfolding, as the world's attention is in many ways turned to what the Mother of God said there in 1917.

The storms that have raged in the world and within the Church in our time can be met with a joyous heart when one takes refuge in the Immaculate Heart of our Mother. The Mother's heart calls us to pray for, to help and defend, the Vicar of Christ, the Pope. At times of darkness, the Pope remains a shining light, speaking for Jesus, and reflecting the love and mercy revealed in the Immaculate Heart of the Mother of the Church.

Since the apparitions of 1917, the "dogma of faith" has indeed been disturbed in many parts of the world. Infidelity has broken out even within the Church, while the Pope has stood, often almost as a single voice, speaking for Jesus Christ. Yet a victory is promised: "In the end, my Immaculate Heart will triumph."

The three children of Fatima each had a special role in conveying to the world the message of Fatima. Jacinta's role, we may say, was to be a victim and model of reparation. Francisco's role was to be the contemplative mystic of the message. Lucia's role has been that of an apostle and evangelist of the message.

Praying the Rosary daily is important, but that is not the only important part of the Fatima message. Sister Lucia has indicated more than once that the most important part of living the Fatima message is *being true to the duties of one's state in life*. It means, in other words, the performance in faith and love of one's *daily duty*.

Made public on April 20, 1946, was a letter written by Sister Lucia to the Bishop of Gurza, in which she spoke clearly of the need to assimilate penance into one's daily life: "The penance which God now asks is this: The sacrifice which each person has to impose on himself in order to lead a life of justice is the observance of His law. He wishes this way to be made known to souls with clearness, for many consider the meaning of the word *penance* to be great austerities, and, not feeling strength or generosity for such, become discouraged and remain in a life of tepidity and sin. Between Thursday and Friday, at 12 o'clock at night, being in the chapel with the permission of my Mother Superior, our Lord said to me: 'The sacrifice of each one requires the fulfilment of duty and the fulfilment of my law; this is the penance that I now ask and exact.'"

Years ago, when the assistance of Sister Lucia was sought in "reducing" the message of Fatima to a simple formula that all could grasp and live by, she endorsed the following pledge:

Dear Queen and Mother, who promised at Fatima to convert Russia and bring peace to all mankind, in reparation to your Immaculate Heart for my sins and the sins of the whole world, I solemnly promise: (1) To offer up every day the sacrifices demanded by my daily duty; (2) to say part of the Rosary (five decades) daily while meditating on the Mysteries: (3) to wear the Scapular of Mt. Carmel as profession of this promise and as an act of consecration to you. I shall renew this promise often, especially in moments of temptation.

People have become so removed from the spirit of sacrifice in observing the duties of their various states in life that, when temptations come, they often run away from their duty rather than face reality and accept that burden, motivated by love of God and neighbor. In the case of marriage, the spirit of sacrifice means carrying the burden together, as husband and wife. But the spirit of the times encourages us all to seek comfort and to avoid pain, effort, penance, and whatever is difficult.

Pope John Paul II, in a papal letter addressed "to all the priests of the Church on the occasion of Holy Thursday" after his election, called for their loyalty to the duties of their state in life. The Pope asked that emphasis be placed on lifelong fidelity in the priestly vocation. He urged priests to call on their resources of faith and prayer in moments of crisis, "and not have recourse to a dispensation" from their priestly functions.

To remain true to one's state in life, performing one's daily duty, one needs to live a life of prayer. Pope John Paul II, in announcing that he prays the Rosary to help him make major decisions, shows the right understanding of the importance of the Rosary and its ability to gain him spiritual strength for the fulfillment of his call to daily duty.

Heroic acts and sacrifices of short duration are praised by the world. The fulfillment of daily duty, year after year, in every state in life requires much heroism too, for which God has promised sufficient grace for those who will cooperate with His holy will. The world may never sing the praises of those who are faithful to their daily duties, but heaven has promised them an eternal, imperishable crown, as well as peace of heart in this life.

Fatima is truly a "time capsule of our future." What our Lady predicted in 1917 has gradually been unfolding. As we approach the end of the second millenium of Christianity, the world can better rediscover the meaning of Fatima, and thus respond to the Immaculate Heart of Mary. I say "the world," because the call of heaven made at Fatima was not only to Catholics, but to everybody.

Our divine and loving Savior, through His Mother, has asked for human cooperation. The message of the Virgin at Fatima is a "reaffirmation of the Gospels" (Pope Pius XII) unfolding for us the "graces and mercy" that heaven offers us through the intercession of her Immaculate Heart. The baneful influence everywhere of the "errors of Russia," of which she spoke, is obvious to all whose eyes are open to truth. The world can yet recognize that Fatima is indeed what Pope John XXIII said it is: "the hope of the world."

Fatima Prayers

Taught by the Angel of Peace (1916)

O my God, I believe, I adore, I trust, and I love you. I beg pardon for those who do not believe, do not adore, do not trust, and do not love you.

(Three times.)

O most holy Trinity, Father, Son, and Holy Spirit, I adore you profoundly. I offer you the most precious Body, Blood, Soul, and Divinity of Jesus Christ, present in all the tabernacles of the world, in reparation for all the outrages, sacrileges, and indifference by which He is offended. Through the infinite merits of the Sacred Heart of Jesus and the Immaculate Heart of Mary, I beg the conversion of poor sinners. *(Three times.)*

Taught by Our Lady of Fatima (1917)

O most holy Trinity, I adore you. My God, my God, I love you in the Most Blessed Sacrament. *(Adoration prayer.)*

O my Jesus, forgive us our sins, save us from the fires of hell, lead all souls to heaven, especially those in most need of your mercy.

(To be said after each decade of the Rosary.)

O my Jesus, this [act of sacrifice] is for love of you, for conversion of sinners, and in reparation for the offenses committed against the Immaculate Heart of Mary. *(Sacrifice prayer: to be said when making a sacrifice.)*

Sources of Additional Information

Fatima in Lucia's Own Words [Memoirs], by Sister Lucia de Jesus (Santos). Stella Maris Books, P.O. Box 11483, Fort Worth, Texas 76110.

The Marian Catechism, by Rev. Robert J. Fox. Our Sunday Visitor, Inc., 200 Noll Plaza, Huntington, Indiana 46750.

Fatima Today, by Rev. Robert J. Fox. Christendom Publications, Box 87, Route 3, Front Royal, Virginia 22630.

The Call of Heaven: Brother Gino, Stigmatist, by Rev. Robert J. Fox. Christendom Publications.

Fatima: The Great Sign, by Francis Johnston. Ave Maria Institute, Washington, New Jersey 07882.

The Secret of Fatima, by Joaquin Maria Alonso, C.M.F. The Ravengate Press, Cambridge, Massachusetts 02138.

Fatima from the Beginning, by Rev. John de Marchi, I.M.C. Edições: Missões Consolata, Fatima, Portugal.

Soul, bi-monthly magazine, Ave Maria Institute, Washington, New Jersey 07882.